David Glasgow Farragut

Courageous Navy Commander

by Leila Merrell Foster

Consultant: Charles Abele, Ph.D.
Social Studies Instructor (Ret.)
Chicago Public School System

CHILDRENS PRESS®
CHICAGO

PICTURE ACKNOWLEDGMENTS

Historical Pictures Service, Chicago—pages 59 (top)

North Wind Picture Archives—pages 2, 34, 44, 53 (2 photos), 54-55, 56 (3 photos), 57 (2 photos), 58 (3 photos), 94, 98

UPI/Bettmann Newsphotos—pages 59 (bottom), 60

Karen Yops—map on page 6

Cover illustration by Len W. Meents

ACKNOWLEDGMENTS

All quotations from David Glasgow Farragut's Journal and letters used in this book come from: *The Life of David Glasgow Farragut, First Admiral of the United States Navy, Embodying His Journal and Letters,* by his son, Loyall Farragut (New York: D. Appleton and Company, copyright 1879). Substantial sections of Farragut's Journal and letters can be found in *David Glasgow Farragut: Admiral in the Making,* by Charles Lee Lewis (Annapolis: United States Naval Institute, copyright 1941) and *David Glasgow Farragut: Our First Admiral,* by Charles Lee Lewis (Annapolis: United States Naval Institute, copyright 1943). All other quotes are as attributed in the text.

Library of Congress Cataloging-in-Publication Data

Foster, Leila Merrell.
   David Glasgow Farragut: courageous naval commander/by Leila M. Foster.
   p. cm.—(People of distinction)

   Includes bibliographical references and index.
   Summary: Describes the life and career of the distinguished officer who became the first admiral in the United States Navy.
ISBN 0-516-03273-9
   1. Farragut, David Glasgow, 1801-1870—Juvenile literature.
2. Admirals—United States—Biography—Juvenile literature.
3. United States. Navy—Biography—Juvenile literature. 4. United States—History, Naval—To 1900—Juvenile literature.
[1. Farragut, David Glasgow, 1801-1870. 2. Admirals.] I. Title.
II. Series.
E467.1.F23F67   1991   940.54'5973'092—dc20   [B]

                                      91-8031
                                         CIP
                                         AC

Table of Contents

Chapter 1
The Battle for Mobile Bay 7

Chapter 2
Son of Spain, Boy of the American Frontier 19

Chapter 3
The Nine-Year-Old Midshipman 27

Chapter 4
To War 35

Chapter 5
The Last Battle of the *Essex* and the
End of the War 45

Chapter 6
The Navy at Peace 61

Chapter 7
Lieutenant at Last 69

Chapter 8
Best Union Officer of the Civil War 81

Glossary 95

Index 104

ALABAMA

Tensaw River

Mobile River

Chickasaw

Prichard

Mobile

Mobile Bay

• Fairhope

Bon Secour Bay

FORT GAINES

DAUPHIN ISLAND

FORT MORGAN

MOBILE POINT

□ Confederate fleet
− Union fleet
▲ Torpedoes
× Pilings off Dauphin Island

Gulf of Mexico

The start of the Battle of Mobile Bay, August 5, 1864

Chapter 1

THE BATTLE FOR MOBILE BAY

"Damn the torpedoes! Full speed ahead." Admiral David Glasgow Farragut shouted down these orders from the rigging of his flagship where he had climbed to get a better view of the battle. This command, given around 8:00 A.M. on August 5, 1864, was to turn a likely defeat of the Union navy into the decisive victory over the Confederate forces in the Civil War battle in the bay of Mobile, Alabama.

Farragut was a first-generation American. His father was of Hispanic heritage, and was born in the Balearic Islands of Spain. The family came from a seafaring tradition that stretched back to the great Spanish navy, the Armada, that threatened England in 1588. His mother was of Irish ancestry. Farragut was the first person appointed to the rank of admiral in the navy of the United States. President Abraham Lincoln considered Farragut the best appointment in either the army or the navy.

Naval warfare was to change radically because of the fighting in the Civil War. Torpedoes (called mines today) had not been widely used before because of public horror at what they could do and because of imperfections in the design and construction of their gunpowder containers. The Confederates, however, improved this weapon so that torpedoes became a deadly threat. Sometimes beer kegs were filled with powder and fitted with a fuse, or primer, that would explode when contact was made with a ship. Underwater explosives were an important Confederate weapon, respected by the Union sailors for the damage they could do to their ships.

Another radical change was the introduction of some ironclad ships to fight the ones made of wood. A Union wooden frigate, the *Merrimac*, was sunk on April 1, 1861 when the Union had to evacuate the navy yard at Portsmouth, Virginia. The Confederates, acting under orders of their Navy Secretary Stephen Mallory, who wanted an armored ship, raised the *Merrimac*, covered it with iron, and renamed it the *Virginia*. On March 8, 1862 the *Virginia* sank two Union ships at Hampton Roads, Virginia. The next day the *Virginia* returned and had to confront a Union ironclad, the *Monitor*. The two ships battled but neither won and the battle ended in a draw. It changed naval warfare. Although the Confederate's ship had been renamed *Virginia*, the battle is remembered as the battle between the *Monitor* and the *Merrimac*.

Newly designed ironclad ships had been developed by John Ericsson for the Union navy and launched in 1862 to face the tall wooden sailing ships used by the Confederates. The Union's ironclads had a deck that was usually only about eighteen inches above the water. On the deck was a revolving turret carrying two 11-inch guns. They were called monitors after the famous Union ship, the *Monitor*. The *Monitor* had been described by Confederate Lieutenant James H. Rochelle as "an immense shingle floating on the water, with a gigantic cheese box rising from its center; no sails, no wheels, no smokestacks, no guns."

In 1864 monitors had been in use for only a few years. Many problems remained about their place in warfare strategy. Farragut wrote to his wife: "This question has to be settled, iron versus wood, and there never was a better chance to settle the question as to the seagoing qualities of ironclad ships. We are to-day ready to try anything that comes along, be it wood or iron, in reasonable quantities." The ironclads were like turtles — well protected but slow moving. The wooden ships were fishlike — able to dart around with speed the monitors could not equal.

The Union navy had attempted to blockade with ships outside the Confederate ports to prevent supplies from reaching the Confederate forces. Farragut had been ordered to Mobile, one of the two major ports controlled by the South. He had been thorough in his survey of the bay, his assessment of the Confederate defenses on land and sea, and his request for additional ships and improved ammunition.

The greatest threat from the Confederates was the ironclad named the *Tennessee*. Launched a year earlier at Selma, she was 209 feet long and 48 feet wide. The sides of her battery casemate sloped at a thirty-three degree angle so that shot and shell would bounce off. She was armored with five or six inches of iron plate. The ram with which she could hit other ships stuck out two feet and was covered with iron plates. She had two 7-inch rifles on pivots and four fixed, 6.4-inch rifles. However, the Confederates, who were short on equipment, had to use engines taken from a steamboat and could generate only enough power to drive the *Tennessee* at six knots.

The Confederate navy also boasted four other ships with rams, less heavily armored. Three other gunboats were part of the flotilla. The largest of these was 200 feet long and had two 7-inch rifles and four 32-pound guns.

On the land, Fort Morgan and Fort Gaines guarded the main entrance to the bay, some thirty miles south of the city of Mobile. Between the two forts torpedoes, marked by buoys, had been strung to reduce the channel to just 250 yards directly under the guns of Fort Morgan. There also were some natural defenses—the shallowness of the water and a sandbar just 9 feet beneath the surface near the city.

Farragut made his plans to battle these forces. He outlined a strategy for his fleet. His requests for ironclads had been honored by Washington, but the *Manhattan*, *Winnebago*, *Chickasaw*, and *Tecumseh* were slow in arriving. He had to wait for them so long that he worried that the season of yellow fever and hurricanes would overtake them.

When finally he had the monitors also under his command, Farragut ordered his men to make the ships ready for battle.

The top rigging on the wooden ships had to come down. Wheel positions and machinery on deck were given special protection. In order to provide a defense from round shot and some shell, the sheet chains were hung over the sides of the ships. Starboard boats on the ships were taken off their normal positions. Fourteen wooden ships were paired to form a double column of seven. Farragut had planned to lead his fleet into battle, but only one of his ships, the *Brooklyn*, could deal best with the torpedoes. She had a sweep apparatus to locate the torpedoes and four chase guns to explode them. Farragut decided to let the *Brooklyn* take the lead. The *Brooklyn* was under the command of Captain James Alden, the only commander who had been with Farragut in his earlier battle at New Orleans. Farragut would be on his flagship, the *Hartford*, and it would be second in line. Of the other officers with Farragut in this battle, a surprising number, like Farragut himself, had been Southerners by birth but had elected to fight in the Union forces.

The attack was to be made at low speed on the morning tide when the wind was from the west-southwest and would blow the smoke into the eyes of the defending Confederates. Once past the forts and into the bay, the ironclads would take on the *Tennessee* and the other Confederate ironclads. The gunboats, armed boats that could go into shallower water, would attack the Confederate gunboats. Seven ships would help the army forces they carried to land on the beach to take the forts and confront the Confederate ground troops.

For the Confederates, led by Admiral "Buck" Buchanan, the coming battle was crucial for the Southern navy. The Confederacy had to break through the blockade that was cutting off vital supplies for the war effort. Most of the Confederate sailors were freshwater, not saltwater, trained. Some were soldiers who had been forced into service in the navy. However, the Confederates had demonstrated that they would fight bravely as they had in the past on the Mississippi River.

Thursday, August 4, was a long day. One of the Union monitors, the *Tecumseh*, had arrived at the Pensacola, Florida, base in need of repairs and was the last to join Farragut's fleet. She arrived at about 5:00 P.M. on the afternoon before the battle. Rain pelted the ships about sunset, but then the weather began to clear and the desired southwest wind came up. Farragut announced that they would fight the next day. That night a comet streaked across the sky—an omen of victory according to the superstition of the sailors.

At 4:00 A.M., the wooden ships began forming into a double line. At 5:30 after finishing his breakfast and getting the latest evaluation of the weather, Farragut said to his fleet captain that they might as well get under way. The signal was passed along to the other ships in the flotilla. The double column of wooden ships with the four monitors to the right of them moved forward.

The Confederates observed the movement and the signals

aboard the Union ships and took their battle position in a single line across the channel. The port guns of the Confederate ships were trained on the Union fleet.

At 6:47, the Union monitor *Tecumseh* opened fire on Fort Morgan and the fort fired back. For half an hour the fleet was under fire from the fort, but it was a sweeping fire that did little damage. Farragut climbed up into the port main rigging of his ship so that he could see the positions of all the vessels of his fleet. As the smoke became thicker, the admiral went higher up. The fleet captain, seeing the exposed position of the admiral, sent a sailor up with a line to secure the admiral so that he would not fall to the deck, unless the lines gave way.

At first the battle was largely noisy but without much damage. Guns boomed. Shots whined through the air. There was firing from the Union ships, the forts, and the Confederate ships. However, the Confederates began to get a more accurate firing range and the *Hartford*, carrying the blue pennant that indicated the admiral was on board, became the most important target.

Then a message was sent from the *Brooklyn* to the *Hartford* that the Union monitors had moved left and were directly ahead. The *Brooklyn* could not go on without passing them. Captain Alden was asking for orders. Although the general orders covered this situation, Farragut signaled for him to go ahead according to plan. The general orders also had covered instructions not to pass to the west of the buoys marking the torpedoes. However, Captain Craven of the monitor *Tecumseh* was afraid that the *Tecumseh* would run aground in the shallows. He slowed the passage of the wooden ships, struck a torpedo, and sunk the *Tecumseh.*

Captain Alden signaled: "Our best monitor has been sunk." "*Tecumseh* sunk" would have been a shorter message, but Captain Alden's morale was shaken by the loss of what he considered the best hope against the *Tennessee.* Even worse was the effect on the sailors on the other monitors.

The *Tecumseh* went down so quickly that the next monitor in line, the *Manhattan,* could not reverse its course and passed directly over the spot where fellow sailors were floundering in the whirlpools left by the sunken ship. Some of the survivors were able to get away in a boat from the *Tecumseh* and in another boat sent out from the admiral's ship. The Confederates on the *Tennessee* had their guns trained on the *Tecumseh* but were ordered not to fire on the struggling survivors. They raised their guns to aim at ships down the line. The gunners at the fort also withheld fire.

Then the battle resumed. Farragut signaled to Alden: "Tell the monitors to go ahead and then take your place." However, Alden found his ship near the shallow water and saw some buoys indicating that he was off course and perhaps leading the others into a torpedo area. Alden found it difficult to turn out of the way. The other Union ships observed the trouble ahead and their shooting became less accurate. The Confederate firing from the fort became more effective.

At this point Farragut, lashed into his rigging, prayed for God to direct him whether he should go on. He reported that he heard a voice commanding him to "Go on." When he signaled to the *Brooklyn* to ask what was the difficulty, the reply came back "Torpedoes."

Farragut had been regretting the decision not to take the lead position. Now he gave the order to "Damn the torpedoes! Full speed ahead!" The *Hartford* passed the *Brooklyn*. Although the other captains feared that they would meet disaster from the torpedoes, they followed the admiral. Some of the officers reported that they heard the snapping of the primers on the torpedoes, but not a single one was fired. Perhaps the torpedoes had been aimed at the entrance to the bay, and by having to change course, Farragut had led his fleet into the bay at the one point that would be safe to enter. Or perhaps the salt water had corroded the mechanisms of the torpedoes.

The *Tennessee* now focused on the ship flying the admiral's pennant. It moved ahead to sink the *Hartford*. The Union ship was too fast. The *Hartford* passed the *Tennessee*, firing at the monitor until it was in position to engage other Confederate ships. All the other Union ships got past the *Tennessee* except the last one in the column of seven. That unlucky one was damaged by fire from the fort and the monitor. It had to be towed out of danger.

The Union monitors had been waiting for the wooden ships

to go through the passage and had tried to protect them from ramming by the *Tennessee*. Now they were free to turn their fire on the Confederate monitors. An oncoming storm, a northwest squall of wind and rain, closed in.

At 8:35 A.M. the *Hartford* anchored in the middle of the bay. The Union sailors cheered their admiral as they passed his flagship. The Confederate ships scattered to safety under the guns of their fort or were caught by Union vessels. One of the Confederate captains was forced to surrender to the Union captain who had been one of his oldest prewar friends. The Union captain invited him on board for refreshments.

While his crew enjoyed some rest, Farragut turned his attention to the *Tennessee* that was now safe under the guns of the fort. That ship had sustained a hundred hits from the broadsides of the Union ships, but no serious damage had been done to her iron sides or to her machinery. She had been slowed down because of damage to the smokestacks. However, as long as she could move, she was a threat.

The Confederate Admiral Buchanan ordered the *Tennessee* to shoot off all its ammunition to do as much damage to the Union fleet as possible and then retire back to the safety of the guns of the fort. Farragut, before he saw the *Tennessee* approach, had planned to wait until that evening when it was dark and then to board one of his monitors and lead the attack of his monitors against the Confederate ship. Now he ordered his fleet to fighting readiness.

The Union ship, the *Monongahela*, attacked the *Tennessee* at full speed and carried away the entire iron prow of her prey. Next the *Lackawanna* rammed the *Tennessee* so hard that the two ships swung head and stern to each other. The *Hartford* was the third to attack. While Farragut climbed into the rigging to watch the action, a lieutenant tried to pull him down without success. Again he was secured with a line to keep him from falling, and the lieutenant stood with his revolver to pick off anyone on the Confederate ship who might attempt to shoot the admiral. The *Hartford* struck only a glancing blow and then was rammed by one of the Union ironclads. The Union ships surrounding the *Tennessee* had to watch out to avoid hitting each other.

A shell from a Union monitor wounded the Confederate Admiral Buchanan in the leg. Still the Confederates did not surrender. The *Tennessee* sustained great damage. Her wheel chains were shot away. Tackles that had been substituted for steering were damaged. Her casement was shattered and ready to fall off. Commander J.D. Johnston, captain of the *Tennessee*, had been given the option of surrender by his admiral. As the surrender flag was raised, another Union ship was moving in for attack. The Union captain could not stop his motion although he did turn off his engines. After a glancing blow was struck, the Union captain sent a boat for Captain Johnston, who had been an old friend before the war.

Farragut was not so generous in the defeat of Admiral

Buchanan. He did not go on board the *Tennessee* to visit the wounded admiral and receive the Confederate's sword. A junior officer performed that task. Farragut did not easily forgive officers who had been trained by the United States but sided with the Confederacy. Nevertheless, Admiral Buchanan received medical treatment and was sent to a Pensacola hospital along with other wounded.

The battle had lasted about three hours from the time that the fort fired its first gun to the surrender of the *Tennessee*. However, Farragut considered it one of the toughest he had fought. The Union had 52 killed and 170 wounded, not counting the 93 killed from the *Tecumseh* that sank. In addition to that monitor, a supply ship that had not followed orders was lost. Other ships in Farragut's fleet were badly damaged.

The Confederates had twelve killed and twenty wounded. One of their vessels managed to escape on the night following the battle, although it was under fire by Union ships. One of the forts surrendered in two days, the other fought on for another two weeks.

Lincoln wrote his thanks and ordered a special 100-gun salute for Admiral Farragut at every Union navy yard. Farragut was recognized as a great admiral by the British and the French. This hero had not had an easy boyhood or climb up the officer ranks of the American navy. The praise he now received for the battles he fought must have been welcome to one who had to prove his worth.

Chapter 2

SON OF SPAIN, BOY OF THE AMERICAN FRONTIER

The first American admiral was the son of a Spanish sailor and hero of the American Revolution. Jorge Antonio Magin Ferragut was to become known as George Farragut in his adopted country. Born in the Balearic Islands of Spain, the admiral's father came from a distinguished family of soldiers, priests, and bishops. Farraguts had fought to drive the Moors out of Spanish territory, had sailed with the great Spanish Armada, and had drawn the official government maps of Majorca.

George Farragut was sent to Barcelona to school. At the age of ten he joined a ship of the merchant service. By the time he was twenty years old, he was captain of a small merchant ship sailing in the Caribbean between Havana and Veracruz with stops sometimes at New Orleans, then a Spanish territory.

It was at New Orleans in 1775 that he heard of the fighting by the American colonists against the British. Captain Farragut hated England because, although he was a Spaniard by language and family, his home in Minorca had been given to the British by the Treaty of Utrecht in 1713. When Jorge Ferragut was born there in 1755, he became the subject of the British

King George III. France then took over the island while he was still a boy. The Minorcans disliked both of these occupying nations.

When the captain learned the news of the American Revolution, he sailed to Port-au-Prince, Haiti, where he sold his cargo for cannon, muskets, and ammunition and sailed to Charleston, South Carolina, with these valuable supplies. Joining the American forces, he became George Farragut, lieutenant on an American privateer—a privately owned ship that was armed and commissioned by the Americans to attack and capture enemy ships. Soon Farragut was in the navy of South Carolina overseeing the construction of ships. When the navy of that colony was destroyed, he was transferred to the army as commander of a battery of guns taken from a ship. He was captured but exchanged as a prisoner of war and was off again and fighting aboard another privateer sailing from Philadelphia. There he was wounded but later returned to fight in the cavalry in South Carolina.

After the war, Farragut went back to the sea for seven years and then secured an appointment from an old friend, William Blount, who had been appointed governor of the South Western Territory that would be made into the state of Tennessee. Farragut received several land grants amounting to more than six hundred acres and decided that he now had enough assets to consider marriage.

Farragut married Elizabeth Shine in 1795. He was forty

years old and she was thirty. Elizabeth was born in North Carolina and later moved with her family to the territory that was to become Tennessee. Her grandfather had come from Dublin, Ireland, around 1710, and her father and uncle had fought in the North Carolina militia. While George Farragut was brave and charming, it was Elizabeth Shine who had a strength of character that was to see her through the adventures that would come in her married life.

Farragut built a stone and log house in Knoxville where their first child, William, was born in 1797. Then the family moved about fifteen miles to the southwest on the north bank of the Holston River where Farragut was granted a license to keep a public ferry at his landing. It was here that Farragut built another home, forty by twenty feet, larger than most of the frontier cabins. Logs were notched at the four corners and then made airtight with a mixture of clay and grass or moss. Windowpanes were made of paper soaked in hog's fat or bear's grease and were protected by wooden shutters. A heavy door could be made secure, and loop holes in the wall permitted the use of guns in the case of Indian attacks.

It was here that their second son, who was to become the future admiral, was born. He was named James Glasgow Farragut after a family friend who was secretary of state of North Carolina. Later, when he was about twelve years old, he was to change his first name from James to David although he was called Glasgow.

When Glasgow was only five, his older brother nine, his sister Nancy two, and a baby brother George less than a year old, there was an Indian attack. Mrs. Farragut was home alone and caught sight of Indians at a distance. She decided that they looked as though they were going to surround the house. She gathered the children together and put them in the loft of the log kitchen that stood a distance from the house (a precaution against cooking fires getting out of control).

The mother warned the children to be quiet and then went to the main house to attract attention away from the children. The Indians approached and after much conversation said that they would leave if she would give them some whiskey. As she began to open the door, one of the Indians struck at her with a knife. She slammed the door shut, protecting herself from the blow. Then she remained inside the house with an ax as a defense until the Indians left. When finally she felt it was safe to go outside and get the children, she found them frightened but safe, lying still in the kitchen loft. Even fifty years later, the admiral could recount in detail this first adventure.

When George Farragut returned home, he was so angry that he wanted to pursue the Indians by himself right then and there. His wife was able to reason with him that he needed help against so many Indians. He put on his uniform and gathered eight or ten others and they rode off after the intruders. It is not clear whether or not they caught up with them.

George Farragut was restless. Though he was considered a

great Indian fighter and a hunter for food, he may have found the people of Tennessee and the country not as much to his liking as the more Spanish city of New Orleans. While there are reports that he was proficient in the English tongue, his letters show that he lacked skill in writing English. When in New Orleans, he probably visited where Spanish was spoken.

In 1803 after the Louisiana Purchase had made New Orleans an American city, the new governor-general of the territory probably used his influence to gain the appointment of Farragut as a sailing master in the United States navy with duty at New Orleans. The Spanish and French population there were hostile to the new government. A trustworthy man of Spanish descent who could speak other languages would be an asset.

Elizabeth Farragut, who had to leave her Tennessee family behind, would scarcely have shared the enthusiasm for the move. In order to take a family to New Orleans in 1807, a keelboat or flatboat had to be built. The back half of the boat was roofed over to be used as living quarters. Pens for animals were included. Food for family and animals had to be stored, but water could be taken directly from the rivers. Two oars on either side of the boat were used in emergencies. A large oar at the stern was for steering. The river current provided the main power going downstream.

George Farragut did not accompany the family because he had to hurry to New Orleans to take command of *Gunboat No. 13*. Instead, he hired a young Kentuckian named Merrill Brady to take his family the seventeen hundred miles by river to their new home. It would take them at least several months to make the journey.

What thoughts must have gone through the mind of Elizabeth Farragut as she waved good-bye to her family. She was pregnant with her fifth child, who was to be named Elizabeth. Glasgow was then six years old. The family left in early autumn so that they would miss the yellow fever season in the south along the coast. Indian attack was unlikely along the river, but river pirates sometimes preyed on the shipping. The family sailed on the Holston and Clinch rivers, on to the Tennessee, then to the Ohio River, and finally to the Mississippi. The children could have seen Indian villages, herds of buffalo, deer, and flocks of birds such as wild turkey. Other boats on the river increased in number as they reached their destination. Glasgow's first long water voyage was on the Mississippi where later he would win fame.

When they arrived, the Farraguts set about establishing their new home. The site was near the shore of Lake Pontchartrain. On November 12, Elizabeth gave birth to her daughter. But tragedy was to strike the family the next summer.

One summer day in 1808, George Farragut was off duty and went out fishing on the lake. He came across a friend, Sailing Master David Porter, who had just suffered a sunstroke. Farragut took him home and his wife took care of the sick friend. Unfortunately Porter, who was ailing from tuberculosis, died. Mrs. Farragut became ill with what was reported to be yellow fever and died the same day. They both were buried on June 24, 1808 in the Protestant cemetery.

George Farragut was left with five children to rear. His friend's son, Commander David Porter, Jr., who had just arrived several days before the deaths to take charge of the United States Naval Station in New Orleans, tried to help by transferring George Farragut from command of the gunboat to duties within the station. William, the first son, was given an appointment as a midshipman in the navy.

Soon after this George Farragut retired from the navy and purchased a nine-hundred-acre plantation on the Pascagoula River, one hundred miles east of New Orleans.

Commander Porter was still concerned about the family who had been so kind to his father. Porter and his wife offered to care for and educate one of the children. George Farragut recognized that sponsorship by the commander could be an invaluable aid to the career of one of his sons. Still he did not want to see a child leave. Finally he agreed to the plan if the Porters could convince one of the children to accept the offer. Glasgow, now eight years old, jumped at the chance. His brother was already a midshipman, and Glasgow dreamed of a life at sea. One of his sisters also was taken along into the Porter home for a time.

Though never formally adopted, Glasgow was treated like a son by the Porters. Forty years later, the admiral was to write in his Journal: "Thus commenced my acquaintance with the celebrated Commodore David Porter, late of the United States Navy, and I am happy to have it in my power to say, with feelings of the warmest gratitude, that he ever was to me all that he promised, my 'friend and guardian'."

As long as the Porters remained in New Orleans, Glasgow frequently visited his father at the plantation and on excursions on Lake Pontchartrain. Indeed, it was his father who taught him much about boats and seamanship. Considered somewhat reckless by others, the father took his children on a sail from New Orleans to Havana in his pirogue—really a dugout canoe made of two pieces of wood. Also, he would take them out on the lake in gale winds, for he believed childhood was the time for them to conquer their fears.

Glasgow remembered that his very first experience on salt water on Lake Pontchartrain was uncomfortable enough that he had wished it would be his last. However, the children learned how to take care of themselves regardless of the weather. If they were prevented from returning from a trip, they would wrap themselves in the sails or scoop out beds of sand on a beach to keep warm.

On June 21, 1810, Glasgow waved good-bye to his family for good. The Porters were transferred from New Orleans, and Glasgow accompanied his new family. He was never to see his father again. However, a new life for him lay ahead as he became a midshipman at the age of nine.

Chapter 3

THE NINE-YEAR-OLD MIDSHIPMAN

The Porters and Glasgow made the journey to Washington, D.C., on board a bomb ketch, the *Vesuvius*, a small sailing ship that carried eleven small guns and a crew of thirty. A stop was made at Havana so Porter could claim his reward from Spain for the capture of pirates while he was in New Orleans.

A British ship had fired on a United States vessel shortly before the Porters arrived at Havana. Porter, who had a long and distinguished naval career that had involved a number of fights against the British, was furious. Admiral Farragut, who had been too young to be influenced much by the revolution, recalls this incident as the beginning of his dislike of the British. He felt that this insult had to be avenged.

When the family reached Washington, Porter took Glasgow with him when he met with Paul Hamilton, the secretary of the navy. The secretary promised Glasgow a commission as midshipman when he became ten years old. However, the commission from President James Madison came through on December 17, 1810, when Glasgow was just nine and a half.

It was about this time that David Porter gave Glasgow a gold watch that was inscribed: "D.P. to D.G.F., U.S.N." From that time on, Glasgow was known as David Glasgow Farragut.

It was not until he was ten that Glasgow Farragut went aboard a United States ship as a commissioned officer. Porter was to command the frigate *Essex*, one of the newer ships. It was 140 feet long and 37 feet in the beam and carried forty-six guns. Porter stayed on shore while the ship was being refitted, but he sent Glasgow and another young midshipman aboard with a note to the executive officer to look after them. He ordered a wherry (a small boat) to be sent ashore for him each morning under the charge of Midshipman Farragut. It was an important assignment for one so young.

Thus Glasgow, who was short for his age and weighed not more than seventy pounds, was put in command of six sailors. He had to direct the timing and manner of the landing and had responsibility for the order of his crew. One day some of the men on the dock who observed the young lad in his blue uniform with brass buttons waiting with his crew in the captain's wherry could not resist teasing him and pouring the contents of an old water pot on him. One of his crew caught the offending dockhand with a boat hook and dragged him into the boat. The crew and the dockhands got into a brawl. Since Midshipman Farragut was fighting with the rest, he and the others were arrested by the police who moved in to restore order.

When Captain Porter was told of the incident, he seemed more amused than upset. One of his officers had reported that Glasgow was "three pounds of uniform and seventy pounds of fight."

The regular, or undress, uniform as it was called consisted of a short blue coat with a standing collar with a button and a slip of lace on each side, a vest, knee breeches, white stockings, shoes like slippers, and a plain cocked hat. The dress uniform was more elegant. The coat had tails like those of higher ranking officers. There was more gold lace trim and buttons. The shoes had buckles, and the cocked hat was trimmed with gold lace. Glasgow even had a short curved sword. It was this dress uniform that Glasgow wore on the day that Captain Porter took charge of his ship, read the orders from the secretary of the navy, and raised his flag. A band played on this occasion.

Glasgow had a graceful way of carrying himself and a ready smile. He was small for his age. His features showed the mixture of Spanish and Irish blood. His oval face had a somewhat swarthy complexion, his hair was a dark brown, and his eyes were hazel or light brown. He was talkative and enjoyed joking. Sensitive and quick to take offense at injustice, he found it difficult to conceal his emotions.

For a midshipman, the regulations provided only that he had to follow orders, keep a regular journal to be delivered to the commanding officer at stated times, and study naval tactics and seamanship. The journal was to give the young men practice in writing, spelling, and composition. The midshipmen had school that was frequently interrupted by duties around the ship. They had a great variety of tasks—from echoing the orders of the officer of the deck and seeing that they were obeyed to climbing to the top of the boat to superintend work being done.

The midshipmen lived together in the steerage or the "gun room" just ahead of the wardroom. Here their mess (dining) table was fastened to the floor. They slept in hammocks that at night were suspended from hooks attached to the overhead beams. This area was neither well ventilated nor heated. In winter months, for heat they had only buckets of sand in which they buried hot 24-pound shot. There was rarely any privacy but, instead, noise of sailors telling tall tales, singing, playing cards, or playing pranks. Perhaps that was why Glasgow enjoyed climbing to the maintop and sitting up there.

Food in port was good but plain. However, when the ship was at sea, there was hardtack (unsalted biscuits) infested with weevils, tough beef soaked in brine, rice, pork and bean soup, and a hot dish of hardtack baked with pork fat. Even the young midshipmen had a regular ration of grog that the older ones often took from them.

Farragut recorded in his journal the names of the officers with whom he was impressed. He made no reference to the twelve midshipmen with whom he served or the three hundred men in the crew. He probably had to endure a good deal of teasing on his first sailing although, because of his relationship to the captain, the hazing could not go too far. Moreover, the officers had a responsibility of looking after the young men. One lieutenant on the ship told the story years later of finding young Glasgow asleep on night watch leaning against a gun carriage. He covered the young boy with his jacket against the cold air.

By October 25, 1811, the *Essex* had been refitted and weighed anchor. Slowly the ship turned toward Hampton Roads, Virginia. The sails began to fill with wind. It was not long until Glasgow felt the swaying of the deck beneath him. What a beautiful sight it was to see his ship under full sail!

The ship was under orders to protect American commerce from improper and illegal interference. The British had stopped an American ship, boarded her, and removed a native-born American passenger under the pretext that he was British. There had been other fights between ships of the two nations.

Captain Porter lost no time in training his men in the use of the guns. Farragut was assigned, with two or three other midshipmen, to assist a lieutenant in charge of one of the six divisions. Twice a day during good weather, the call of the bugle and drums to "quarters" resulted in the men dropping whatever they were doing, grabbing a cutlass, and rushing as fast as they could to their stations. Sometimes the call would come at night. The men had to get out of their hammocks, stow them away, and get to their stations in about ten minutes. Sometimes fire drills would be practiced at night. Occasionally, the guns would be loaded with powder and cannon balls.

Then there would be great cheering when a target such as a floating cask was hit.

The *Essex* returned to port after a short cruise of a few weeks. After only a week in Norfolk she headed out to sea again, this time for Chester on the Delaware River. Now life at sea was becoming routine for Glasgow. At daybreak, the drums sounded, the night sentries shot off their loaded guns, and the pipes would carry the order for all to be up and about. After work to make the place shipshape, the bells would call the crew to breakfast—7:00 A.M. in the summer but later in the winter. An hour was allowed for breakfast. Then the midshipmen had two hours for school, with heavy emphasis on navigation. If the weather was clear enough they took readings on the sun to figure out the position of the ship. Grog was given out to the crew. After lunch in steerage for the midshipmen, work on the ship began again. Supper was eaten between 4:00 and 5:00 P.M. Then came a time for relaxation until sunset when the flag was hauled down and the band played "Hail Columbia." Bedtime was around 8:00 P.M. in winter and 9:00 P.M. in summer. Throughout the night the striking of the bell each half hour was answered by the sentries announcing: "All's well."

The *Essex* received new orders to proceed to Newport, Rhode Island. On Christmas Eve the ship had dropped anchor near Newport. About 4:00 A.M. a terrible storm with sleet and snow blew in from the northeast. The ship drifted toward shore. Three more anchors were dropped but failed to hold. The ship was blown onto the shore and keeled over at an angle. The rigging was so covered with ice that the mast could not be lowered. The main and mizzen top gallant masts were blown away.

Captain Porter and Lieutenant Downes took turns on lookout, but could stay out for only a few minutes at a time because of the cold. One of the sailors froze to death in his hammock. Men were ordered to stand by with axes in order to cut away the remaining masts, if needed, to prevent the ship from being driven farther onto the banks. At last the wind let up and the ship was saved.

The storm had done great damage to the coast and to other American ships caught in it. The brig *Nautilus* had been forced to throw all her guns overboard in order to save the ship.

At the beginning of 1812, the ship remained in Newport. There was talk of war in the air, and Captain Porter saw that his men trained well for their work. Commodore Rodgers, who headed the Atlantic Coastal Squadron, declared that the *Essex* was the best sailed ship and the best in gunnery in his squadron.

Congress declared war against the British on June 18. It took two days for the news to reach New York. The squadron put out to search for British ships. Because the *Essex* needed a new foremast, the ship was not ready for action until July 3, just two days before Glasgow's eleventh birthday.

Sailors rounding Cape Horn at the tip of South America
usually faced dangerous seas and bad weather.

Chapter 4

TO WAR

Britain, the great naval power, controlled the seas. The American strategy was to inflict as much damage as possible on British shipping and forces without losing United States ships.

Captain Porter took the *Essex* out of port and set a course toward Bermuda. Within a week, they sighted a convoy of seven British troop transports. Under the cover of darkness, Porter isolated the last of the British ships, a brig, and boarded and captured it. The British officers jeered the Americans, telling them that they were afraid to take on the British frigate that was guarding the convoy. They underestimated the strength of Porter's dislike of the British and the spirit with which the *Essex* crew greeted the idea of a fight.

Porter moved his ship within gunshot of the British frigate, the *Minerva*, and expected that this challenge would result in fighting. Instead the *Minerva* turned and fled through the convoy. The crew wanted to attack the convoy, but Porter sought a fight, not the job of herding the convoy with prisoners back to port.

After removing all the arms from the British brig, Porter forced the officers and men to declare that they would not fight against the United States. They promised to pay a ransom rather than be captured or sunk. While this ransom would not be paid during the war, it was the subject for claims at the end of the war. With this, Porter set the ship free and continued his harassment of shipping. Six more ships were captured in the next two weeks. When they carried cargo that was valuable, they were sent to American ports. Otherwise, prisoners were taken and the ships were burned, or the ships were ransomed by their captains.

Midshipman Farragut played an important role in the incident involving the British ship, the *Alert*. This British man-of-war was fooled at first by the common practice of flying the British flag from the mast of the *Essex* and the other American ships. That way the Americans avoided British warships and lured British merchant ships to them. When the British flag was hauled down and the Stars and Stripes raised, the British captain of the *Alert* fired on the *Essex*. However, he was outmaneuvered by Porter.

The British captain surrendered because of a hole the Americans had blasted in his ship below the waterline, raising the danger of sinking. The *Alert* was the first British man-of-war to be taken by the United States in the War of 1812. The British officers and the crew of the small boat that brought them to the *Essex* were taken on board. Since Captain Porter had other British officers and men on board from his other engagements, it was difficult to keep as close watch on the prisoners as was desirable.

Midshipman Farragut, asleep in his hammock that night, woke up with a start to see someone standing beside him. In the dim light, Glasgow made out the face of the British coxswain of the boat from the *Alert*. The sailor was staring at the midshipmen to see if any were awake. If the coxswain had caught any awake, he would have strangled or run his sword through the young men. Glasgow pretended he was asleep until the man left. Then he crept up to the cabin of Captain Porter to tell him of what he had seen. Porter immediately realized the risk to the ship with the prisoner loose and called out "Fire!" The crew of the *Essex* who had been carefully drilled to man their stations in the event of fire responded promptly. Marines and armed sailors were sent to make the prisoners secure. Farragut's quick thinking and courage helped to save the ship.

After ten weeks at sea, the *Essex* put in at Delaware Bay to resupply the ship. It was September 15, and Porter and Farragut were close enough to visit the Porter home, which they had seen last just before Christmas of the previous year. What tales they had to tell the Porter family! Farragut loved the adventure and excitement. He had made friends among the midshipmen and had become the life of the group, full of fun and pranks. No one could beat him in a race to the top of the mast, and he loved to sit up in the ship's rigging.

After only three days in port, Porter read a Philadelphia paper that carried the news that had been brought by an

American passenger who had been captured and released by a British frigate, the *Southampton*. The British captain, Sir James Yeo, challenged Captain Porter to have a meeting anywhere between the Capes Delaware and Havannah, along the East Coast, where he would be pleased to break a sword over Porter's head and put him in irons. Porter replied accepting this invitation to meet, pledging that no other American ship would interfere with their one-on-one fight, and announcing that the *Essex* would be known by her flag carrying the motto, "Free trade and sailors' rights." The *Essex* put out to sea and cruised around the entrance to the Delaware, but Sir James and the *Southampton* were not to be found.

Porter received orders to bring the *Essex* to rendezvous with another American ship, to continue raiding British ships in the Atlantic that were coming from Africa, and then to cross over into the South American shipping lanes. After that, the two ships might go into the Pacific to destroy the British whaling industry. The strategy was aimed at doing as much harm to commerce as possible and at trying to avoid duels with British warships, because the Americans had a much smaller force. If the *Essex* missed the other American ship, as happened, the orders authorized Porter to proceed alone.

When the ship crossed the equator, Farragut was initiated into the Noble Order of Neptune by having soap and a terrible smelling paste shaved off his face with a wooden razor while he was sitting over a tub of water. After being ducked in the water, he was declared a shellback, or old sailor.

Glasgow also suffered some discipline at the hands of Captain Porter, who discovered the midshipman chewing tobacco. Porter put his hand over Glasgow's mouth and ordered the midshipman to swallow. That was enough for Glasgow for life. He did not like any form of tobacco thereafter.

The *Essex* found good pickings among the British ships. She captured a British ship carrying $55,000 in gold and silver; this ship was then sailed back to the United States by American officers. However, supplies aboard the *Essex* were growing short, and it was not safe to put into port in South America—for fear of being blockaded there. Porter decided to go around Cape Horn and into the Pacific Ocean. The men were put on short rations of bread.

Cape Horn has a reputation for dangerous seas and bad weather. The *Essex* experienced them both. Farragut wrote in his journal: "Large quantities of water rushed down the hatchways, leading those below to imagine that the ship was sinking. This was the only instance in which I ever saw a regular good seaman paralyzed by fear at the dangers of the sea." However, they got around the cape and put into Valparaiso, now in Chile but then a Spanish territory, for supplies.

After leaving Valparaiso, they captured several British whaling ships. The prompt surrender of one of them surprised the *Essex* crew until they discovered that it was manned largely by American seamen who had been forced into service on the

British ship. One of the British ships was converted into an armed vessel to protect the American whalers who worked the area. Porter sailed on to the Galapagos Islands to replenish supplies.

The Galapagos Islands are some 500 miles west of the coast of Ecuador and just south of the equator. They were used as a resupply point for ships in the area. Here the crew, as was the custom of the times, went out on seal hunts. Once they even took on a sea lion. Glasgow did not like the looks of this larger animal and decided to wait out the fight in a boat. The crew led by Captain Porter tried to surround the animal, but when the sea lion had enough of their foolishness, he charged through the circle and headed for the water. Glasgow let out a hearty laugh. The captain retorted that Glasgow was afraid to stand on the beach. Glasgow replied that he did not undertake anything that he did not know how to accomplish.

The Galapagos meant fresh water from springs on the island, fresh meat from the many terrapins there, and new delicacies like the prickly pear. Many years later, Farragut recalled: "These were among the happiest days of my life."

On the way from the Galapagos Islands, the *Essex* captured a number of other ships and had them in tow as prizes of war. Up to this time there had been surprisingly little loss of life on the *Essex*. Some crew members had fallen from the rigging of the ship and had been killed. The surgeon aboard the ship had died of consumption. A few had died from other causes. However, with so many prize ships to get to port Captain Porter faced a decision about allocating responsibility for this task among his officers.

Porter ordered Farragut to be the prize master of the ship called the *Barclay*. Farragut was only twelve years old. He commented: "This was an important event in my life, and when it was decided that I was to take the ship to Valparaiso, I felt no little pride at finding myself in command at twelve years of age." The captain and the first mate of the *Barclay* were to stay on board and to navigate the ship, but Farragut was in charge of the prize crew.

Captain Randall of the *Barclay* did not like the idea of his ship being taken into port because he wanted to continue his whaling business. So when young Farragut was on deck the day the ships were to leave in a convoy, Captain Randall announced that he was taking over command. Farragut ordered the captain to have the main topsail filled so that the ship could move into position in the convoy. Captain Randall said he would shoot any man who touched a rope without his orders. He then went below to get his pistols. Farragut immediately called one of his crew he trusted, explained the situation, and ordered the main topsail filled. The crew member responded: "Aye, aye, sir!" Farragut gave all the necessary orders to get his ship under sail. He sent word to Captain Randall that if Randall came on deck with his pistols, he would put the captain overboard.

As the *Barclay* joined the American ship in charge of the convoy, Farragut and Captain Randall went aboard to report the incident. The captain made light of the matter saying that he had only intended to frighten the boy. Farragut replied: "Captain Downes, ask him if he thinks he succeeded; to show him that I do not fear him I am ready to go back to the ship and proceed with him to Valparaiso." Downes praised Glasgow and told him to resume his command, with Captain Randall as his adviser only if Farragut became separated from the other American ships.

After this adventure, the Americans set off to the Marquesas in search of more British prize ships. Once there, the Americans became involved in some fighting between several local tribes in an effort to bring some peace to the area. Also, the *Essex* was outfitted with a new topmast. After provisions were removed from the ship, some fifteen hundred rats were exterminated. They were smoked out with charcoal fires. The young officers were removed to the chaplain's ship to protect them from the temptations of the South Seas: there they continued their studies. Farragut also learned from the young boys of the island how to throw a spear, to walk on stilts, and to swim better.

The discipline of Captain Porter was tested by a few of the crew who did not want to leave the attractions of the South Sea islands. One of the men, an Englishman who had joined the *Essex* from one of the captured ships, was ordered off the ship and the rest responded to the captain's command to set sail back to the South American coast. On the way there, Porter drilled his crew in the use of guns and small arms. It was well that he did because the *Essex* was sailing to what would be her last fight.

After his mother's death, David Glasgow Farragut went to live with Commander David Porter's family. Farragut began as a midshipman under the command of Porter (above).

Chapter 5

THE LAST BATTLE OF THE *ESSEX* AND THE END OF THE WAR

In Valparaiso, Captain Porter learned that a squadron of British ships had left Rio de Janeiro for the Pacific to give more protection to British shipping there. However, the British ships had not yet appeared in Valparaiso. Perhaps, some speculated, they had been destroyed trying to round Cape Horn in the always dangerous part of the sea there. However, Porter thought that the British might be keeping their arrival in Pacific waters secret so as to better attack the *Essex*.

When two British ships finally came into view, the crew of the *Essex* on shore were recalled to the ship. The *Essex* was made ready for action. The two British ships were larger and could outgun the two American ships. The British frigate was captained by James Hillyar whom Porter knew from a tour in the Mediterranean. Hillyar sailed within ten or fifteen feet of the American ship—closer than was warranted in a neutral port and dangerous in view of the war between the two countries.

Porter warned his old friend that if the British ship should touch the *Essex* there would be bloodshed. Captain Hillyar responded that he had no such intentions, but the jib boom of the British frigate came across the forecastle of the American ship. Porter ordered his crew to be ready to board the British ship as soon as their hulls touched. The British Hillyar apologized for coming so close.

One American crew member who was still under the influence of alcohol thought that one of the British sailors was taunting him. He raised a musket to fire at the offender. An officer saw the problem and decked the sailor before he could fire. If a battle had broken out at this point, the two American ships could easily have destroyed or captured the British frigate in short order due to the vulnerable position of the British.

Captain Hillyar announced that he intended to respect the neutrality of the port. The sailors of both sets of ships were on good terms when on shore. A bit of propaganda warfare took place with the display of mottoes on the flags of the ships. The motto of the *Essex* was "Free trade and sailors' rights." The British ship, the *Phoebe*, raised a flag proclaiming: "God and Country; British sailors' best rights; traitors offend both." Porter replied with another flag: "God, our country and Liberty—tyrants offend them." The sailors composed songs that insulted the other side.

When Hillyar sailed out of the harbor, Porter tried to provoke a fight by taking out one of Porter's prize ships and burning it. However, the British did not want to engage in a one-on-one fight, although they had superior gun power. Instead Captain Hillyar waited until it was two ships against one.

Porter led an expedition of all the small boats of the American ships to try to board the British ship outside the harbor. However, when the Americans came close enough one night they discovered that the British were all set for the attack. Without the element of surprise, the operation had to be canceled.

Concerned that more British reinforcements might join the two ships already in the vicinity of Valparaiso, Porter had decided to try to run the blockade that the British ships were trying to impose outside the harbor. Valparaiso Bay is not enclosed but is an indentation along the long coastline of Chile.

On March 28, 1814, a storm from the south caused the chain on one of the anchors of the *Essex* to break. In order to prevent the ship from being dragged ashore by the other anchor, Porter ordered his crew to put up the sails with the hope of outrunning the British ships. Unfortunately a squall struck. The Americans tried to lower the sails, but the yards jammed and they could not get the canvas down. The ship was forced over until the gunwale was almost under water. The main topmast was lost along with many of the sailors who were manning it. There was no way that the *Essex* could return to pick up the crew who were overboard.

Porter tried to return to his anchorage in the bay, but he was unable to do so with the British in pursuit. Instead he anchored in a small bay near the harbor about a quarter of a mile offshore and three-quarters of a mile from a small battery.

Under international law, the neutral zone of a country extended three miles or the distance of a cannon shot from shore. Porter should have been safe in the bay—especially since Hillyar had given previous assurances that he would respect the neutrality of Chile. However, Hillyar, seeing the *Essex* badly damaged, decided to destroy the enemy ship.

Farragut reported his feelings at seeing the British ships close in for the kill. He knew that their situation was hopeless, but he felt that he and the entire crew would rather die than surrender.

The two British ships opened fire just before 4:00 P.M. and kept up the fight for half an hour before they retired to survey the damage that the battered *Essex* was able to inflict with her guns. When the British returned but stayed outside the range of the American guns that could be operated, Porter decided to try to carry the fight to the British and secure better position by using the one sail that he could still hoist. Now the firing of guns was especially heavy, but the *Essex* could not match the guns of the two British ships.

During this phase of the battle, Midshipman Farragut served as captain's aide, quarter gunner, powder boy, and just about anything else that was needed. He reported the strong impression made on him by the death of the first seaman to fall near him. The man's abdomen was blown away. Soon men were dying all around him, so that even when later he was spattered by the brains of another crew member, it did not make as much of an impression as the first death he witnessed.

Once when Farragut was standing near Porter, the captain received a report that a gunner had deserted his post. The captain ordered Farragut: "Do your duty, sir." That was an order to kill the deserter on sight. Farragut picked up a pistol and went in search of the offender. However, the deserter had escaped with six others in a boat during the fighting and was nowhere to be found.

At one point, Farragut was knocked out when a gun captain was hit in the face by an 18-pound shot and collapsed on the midshipman as both fell down the hatch. Another shot took off Farragut's coattail. Farragut lost a number of close friends in this battle.

Porter, with only one other officer on his feet without wounds, ordered the surrender of the ship. Farragut was commanded to find the signal book and throw it overboard. Also, he and another midshipman walked around the deck throwing over all small arms they could find to prevent the British from capturing them. At 6:20 P.M., the American flag was lowered. For ten more minutes, the British continued firing until they noticed that the flag had been lowered. During that period, four men who were standing near Porter were killed.

Farragut went below deck to see if he could be of any assistance to his injured crewmates. At first he felt faint and sick at the sight of the injuries and the men dying, but he pitched in to help. Of the crew of 255, 155 men were wounded, missing

and presumed drowned, or killed. The British, with their superior firepower, lost only 5 dead and 10 wounded on their two ships. In Captain Porter's official report, he praised by name the conduct of his officers during the fight. Midshipman Farragut was included among those who had "exerted themselves in the performance of their respective duties, and gave an earnest of their value to the service."

Now it was Farragut's turn to be a prisoner. As he was taken to the steerage of the British ship, he heard the British midshipmen shouting about a prize pig they had discovered aboard the American ship. The pig was Farragut's own pet named "Murphy." Farragut demanded his private property and attempted to seize Murphy. The older officers, seeing that they could have some sport out of this demand, offered to give him his pig if he fought the British midshipman for it. Farragut agreed, and a circle was formed to watch the match. Since the American's skills were considerably better than his opponent's, Farragut won easily. He reported: "So I took Master Murphy under my arm, feeling that I had, in some degree, wiped out the disgrace of our defeat."

The American sailors were soon paroled, a status that meant that they could not fight in the war again. They were put ashore in Valparaiso. Porter praised the help that his wounded crew received from the ladies of Valparaiso. They saved the lives of many men. Meanwhile, Farragut continued to assist the surgeon in tending to the wounded. Arrangements were made by Porter to ship the American sailors back to an American port. The twelve-year-old Farragut had gained a wealth of experience from his service aboard the great sailing ship, the *Essex*.

Home again on July 7, 1814, just two days after Farragut's thirteenth birthday, the midshipman made his way back to Chester, Pennsylvania, where the Porters lived. Here, it was back to school for Farragut. The courses were not very regular. The pupils were taught orally without the aid of books. In the afternoon, the class went on long walks. The students were drilled like soldiers and were taught to climb and swim. In later years, Farragut was to praise this experience because of all the knowledge he picked up that was useful to him throughout his life.

According to reports from residents of Chester, Farragut was still very short and carried himself very erect so that he had the benefit of all the inches he had. He was not very handsome, but was very sociable and enjoyed being with the young people at the local gathering spot.

Porter denied Farragut's request to join a group of sailors whom he was leading to fight to save Washington. Porter thought Farragut too young for a land war. However, Washington was taken by the British before Porter's unit arrived.

By the end of November 1814, Farragut was notified that he had been "exchanged" so he was no longer on parole. Undoubtedly it was Porter who arranged for Farragut's orders to be assigned to the brig *Spark*. With the loss of American ships at this point in the war, many young officers quit the service because they had no ships to which they could be assigned.

Away from the direct command of Porter, Farragut found himself with a fairly wild bunch of midshipmen who were rarely sober. Farragut joined the others. His naval career was probably saved by the fact that his habits of doing his duty, so ingrained under the command of Porter, were so strong that he went about his tasks even with a terrible hangover. His ship was just about ready to sail when the peace treaty was signed.

Captain Porter's ship, the *Essex*, battled two British ships at Valparaiso in March 1813.

The levee at New Orleans before the Civil War.

THE HULL OF AN AMERICAN MAN-OF-WAR CUT OPEN AMIDSHIPS, FROM STEM TO STERN.

1. Sailors furling Sails.
2. Poop or Quarter-Deck.
3. Bob Stays.
4. Figure Head.

5. Sailors lowering a Cask.
6. Surgical inspection.
7. Captain's Cabin.
8. Dining-Room.

9. Cook's Galley.
10. Midshipmen's Cabin.
11. Sailors' Berth.
12. Exercising the Guns.

13. Officers' Cabins.
14. Dining-Room of Officers.
15. Dressing a Wound.
16. Musket exercise.

17. Sailors' Mess-Room.
18. Mending Sails.
19. Provision Room.
20. Sick Bay or Hospital.

21. Lowering a Boat.
22. Sail and Cordage Room.
23. The Prison.
24. Shot Magazine.

25. Spirit-Room.
26. Powder Magazine.
27. Blocks, Pulleys, etc.

28. General Store Room.
29. Casks and Tanks.
30. Dunnage.

Left: The *Merrimac* was burned and sunk when the Union
had to abandon the navy yard at Portsmouth, Virginia.
Right: The *Merrimac* before and after (top) its conversion
to an ironclad ship, renamed the *Virginia*.

The battle between the *Monitor* and the *Merrimac*

It was Commander Porter's idea to run the forts at the mouth of the Mississippi and capture the city of New Orleans. Below: The capture of New Orleans.

Above left: The letter Farragut wrote just before the Battle of Mobile Bay reads, "I am going into Mobile Bay in the morning if 'God is my leader,' as I hope he is." Above right: Farragut's flagship during the Battle of Mobile Bay was the *Hartford*. Below: Farragut (top right) watches his crew in action during the Battle of Mobile Bay.

Above: In 1867 Farragut commanded a goodwill tour to European countries. Below: An inaugural ball marked the beginning of Lincoln's second term as president.

A photograph of Farragut taken in New Orleans during
the Civil War

Chapter 6

THE NAVY AT PEACE

Soon Farragut received new orders as the captain's aide on the *Independence*, the flagship of Commodore Bainbridge that was to sail to the Mediterranean. The *Independence* carried eighty-four guns. She had three masts and was 190 feet long and 50 feet in the beam. She was a new class of ship that Congress had authorized in order to build a real navy. Although the navy was experimenting with steamships, sailing ships were still considered superior at that time.

Farragut made friends with an older midshipman, William Taylor, who set a good example for him. Farragut left behind the ways of his old crowd: he saw that his future in a naval career was best served by a course other than heavy drinking.

The *Independence* arrived in the Mediterranean after the war with the Barbary pirates had been settled by another American naval squadron led by Commodore Stephen Decatur. The Barbary pirates harassed American ships during the War of 1812. After cruising around the Mediterranean, the *Independence* returned home.

Next Farragut was ordered to the ship *Washington* under the command of Captain Creighton. Creighton ran a very tight ship with strong punishment for minor infractions. Punishment then might involve suffering two or three dozen lashes, being kept from meals for eight or ten hours, or having to sleep on deck for several nights. Because the *Washington* was a ship of the line—a large battleship that could fight in line formation—mutiny was practically impossible. However, the crew was not happy. Although Farragut could praise the seamanship of the officers of this ship, he preferred the approach of Captain Porter who was liked because, though he was strict, he was fair and generous.

Farragut spent his two years aboard this ship studying the courses he would need to advance in a naval career. He also had time to visit places around the Mediterranean. Chaplain Charles Folsom of the *Washington* asked Farragut to go along with him when he was appointed U.S. consul to Tunis. Folsom had been impressed with the change in Farragut during the two years—especially in the attention of the young man to his studies. The chaplain had been in charge of studies on the *Washington* and wanted to help Farragut continue his education. With the blessing of his commanding officer, Farragut was detailed to go with Folsom.

Since Folsom was only twenty-three years old, Farragut may have related to Folsom more as an older brother. Farragut continued his studies of French, Italian, English literature, and mathematics. After some three months of study at Tunis, Farragut became ill. The doctor prescribed a trip on horseback.

Folsom and the French and Danish consuls together with

Farragut set out on the adventure of a trip inland with an armed escort. Travel in that part of the world was risky, and Farragut had occasion to draw his pistol to prevent being clubbed to death. One very hot day of the journey Farragut had either heatstroke or sunstroke, his tongue was somewhat paralyzed and he could not speak properly. However, he recovered the next day but with some long-term damage to his eyesight. He could not use his eyes longer than to read or write a page.

Soon Tunis was to suffer an epidemic of the plague, with hundreds dying each day from the disease. Farragut left Tunis in October to rejoin his squadron, ending his two years with Folsom. Both Folsom and Richard B. Jones, the American consul at Tripoli, saw the leadership potential in Farragut. Jones, in a letter to Folsom, even referred to Farragut as "the young Admiral."

Farragut became an aide to the captain on the *Franklin*. His ship was visited by the emperor of Austria and the king of Naples. Farragut was assigned the task of interpreting for the emperor. All went well except that there was laughter at his expense when Farragut addressed the emperor as mister instead of one of the loftier titles of royalty.

Very important to the eighteen-year-old Farragut was his assignment to the brig *Spark* as an acting lieutenant. Later he became executive officer with duties that meant that he was really in command of the ship. He felt it was very important to be given command as a young man. Persons who were given important positions only late in life, he thought, were more likely to try to avoid responsibility and to fail.

In 1820, Farragut was ordered home to take the examination for the rank of lieutenant. Even the journey home on a merchant ship provided some excitement. Farragut took charge when it was thought that they would be attacked by a pirate ship.

His experience with the examinations was not so happy. He had feared that he might be deficient in mathematics but was confident with all his experience that he would have no trouble with seamanship. One of the reasons that Farragut gained so much experience aboard the *Spark* was the fact that the captain, Christopher Raymond Perry, was often too drunk for duty. Farragut was not tolerant of this weakness because he had overcome his own excessive indulgence of liquor, and he may have spoken about the captain's condition. When Farragut returned for the examinations, he learned that the captain had been brought home to be tried for drunkenness. Perry's brother-in-law, Captain George Washington Rodgers, sent a message to Farragut to discuss the matter, probably with the intent of asking Farragut to remain silent. However, Midshipman Farragut replied to the captain by asking whether the conversation was to be official or whether the captain was coming as a friend of Perry. If the meeting was to be official, Farragut responded, he had nothing to say. If the captain was coming as a friend of Perry, Farragut indicated that he would send a friend to make arrangements for a settlement—in effect, suggesting a duel. Since Rodgers said that his request came in his official capacity, no further action was taken.

Captains were not used to being treated as Midshipman Farragut had dealt with Captain Rodgers. Unfortunately, Captain Rodgers shared lodgings with Captain Samuel Evans who was to be one of Farragut's examiners. It would be reasonable to assume that Evans would know of Rodgers' irritation with the young Farragut and would come to the examination with an unfavorable impression of the midshipman.

Captain Evans maintained that in answering an oral question Farragut had omitted the need to clear away the bow lines in reefing a sail. Farragut, who had heard the necessary orders given many times and had given them himself, stated that he had answered properly but perhaps he had not been heard. Evans felt that the young eighteen-year-old midshipman was impertinent and insolent. The other two examiners dismissed the issue by saying that they had not noticed, but since Evans was so positive the error must have been made. Farragut realized too late that he should have conciliated rather than insulted Evans, but there was nothing to do but leave with tears in his eyes.

Farragut was informed that he had passed in mathematics but was found "otherwise deficient." He applied to take the examinations again. On his next try in 1821, he passed. He was twentieth in a class of fifty-three.

The failure to pass the exam was a bitter lesson in the need for more personal diplomacy. He wrote: "It was a good lesson that has served me much in life although it cost me dearly. It was the hardest blow I have ever sustained to my pride and the greatest mortification to my vanity. I might have deserved a rebuke, as I am told some of the members proposed, but certainly not a punishment that was to last during life."

During this period of uncertainty, Farragut went to Norfolk where he was to meet his future wife, Susan Caroline Merchant. His pay as a midshipman amounted to $19 a month—not enough to help support his sisters now that his father had died and not enough to support a wife. Even though he had passed the examination to be a lieutenant, that success meant that he simply had an opportunity for a promotion.

Although Farragut had requested sea duty, it was two years from his last ship assignment when in May of 1822 he was ordered aboard the *John Adams* that was to take the new American minister to Veracruz, Mexico. On this trip he met General Santa Anna who had just led a revolution in Mexico to establish a nation independent from European powers. Also, he began to learn Spanish. Five months later, Farragut was back in Norfolk.

His next assignment was aboard the *Greyhound,* a small, shallow-draft, sailing schooner assigned the task of hunting pirates in the south. The crew did clean out one cave where the pirates stored their loot. They burned the houses of the pirates. However, their ship did not see as much action as the others in the squadron. Back at their base in Key West, Farragut was to meet his older brother William, now a lieutenant, for the first time in thirteen years. The two served briefly aboard the same ship.

Still a midshipman, Farragut at the age of twenty-three was given his first real command. His duty aboard the *Ferret* was to escort ships through the pirate-infested waters of the Gulf of Mexico. During this assignment, Farragut secured a leave and visited his family in New Orleans, where he saw his sister Nancy again. The pirate hunters were part of what was called the Mosquito Squadron because of the size of the ships and the prevalence of the insect in these waters. Because it was not known then that the mosquito helped to transmit yellow fever, sailors often slept on deck without any netting for protection.

Farragut came down with his first severe attack of yellow fever as his ship was sailing up the Potomac on its return to Washington, D.C. As soon as his ship docked, Farragut was taken to the hospital.

Farragut had hoped that his pirate-hunting assignments would lead to his promotion to lieutenant so that he might marry Miss Merchant in Norfolk. However, when Farragut was recovered sufficiently to travel to Norfolk, the couple decided to get married on September 2, 1824 even though the promotion had not come through. The midshipman took his bride to meet the Porter family, whose home was then near Washington. Finally, after fourteen years as a midshipman Farragut was promoted and commissioned a lieutenant.

Chapter 7

LIEUTENANT AT LAST

The promotion meant that Farragut was now entitled to receive $40 a month when on active service. However, he received only half that amount when the navy did not employ him. It was not until June that he received orders to a ship bound back to the West Indies. Because of his bout with yellow fever, he presented a medical report that stated that he was fit for duty but recommended he stay out of the West Indies where the disease was prevalent.

In August, he was assigned to the frigate *Brandywine*, which was built to transport the great Revolutionary War hero Lafayette home to France after his triumphal tour of the country he had helped to free. This maiden voyage of the ship almost ended as soon as it began because a leak developed where the caulking worked out of the seams. Only the dumping of some of the ammunition and the swelling of the planks as they soaked up the water prevented the ship from having to return to dry dock.

On arrival in France, Lieutenant Farragut was sent ashore to arrange for the general's arrival. There was concern that Lafayette would not be safe because during his absence a new king of France who hated republicanism, Charles X, had come to the throne. However, there was no incident and, after a stop in England to fix the leak, the *Brandywine* set sail for the Mediterranean and spent the winter in the Balearic Islands, the home of Farragut's father.

On Farragut's return to New York in May 1826, he found his wife seriously ill and in much pain from neuralgia. He requested a leave of absence from active service and took his wife to New Haven, Connecticut, to consult a physician there who was becoming known as the best doctor in the United States. The Farraguts spent four months in New Haven. The lieutenant attended lectures given by the professors at Yale College. He was especially interested in the courses on chemistry and mineralogy. Being able to hear lectures was especially valuable for him because, since his sunstroke in Tunisia, he had not been able to read or write more than a page at a time.

Mrs. Farragut apparently obtained only temporary relief and her health continued to decline. When they returned to Norfolk, Farragut was ordered to a receiving ship. The captain allowed Mrs. Farragut to live on board so that the lieutenant could take care of her.

The lieutenant's assignment included setting up a school for boys in the service who could not read or write. The navy was assuming greater responsibility for these young people, and also recognized that the new technology of steam created the need for more educated seamen. The secretary of the navy commended Farragut for his school.

One of his young charges provided a contest of wills. The young man announced that he had run away from home and joined the navy to avoid school and that he had no intention to learn now. Farragut replied that the young man would find the punishment that would be meted out for not learning would be more costly than study. Still the boy was stubborn. Farragut tried encouragement, whipping, and finally settled on ridicule as the most effective weapon.

Years later, a young man introduced himself to Farragut. The same lad who had been so much trouble thanked Farragut for his efforts. The boy had learned enough navigation to be able to bring a ship back to New York when the captain and first mate had died. Later he was made captain of a merchant vessel. Farragut mused that he was determined not to be outwitted by the stubbornness of a fifteen-year-old's attitudes toward learning.

Farragut remained at Norfolk for two years, mainly to care for his wife. But his career in the navy depended on his taking sea duty. In October 1828, he was assigned to the *Vandalia*, a small sloop that set sail for Brazil. On board when a squall hit the ship, Farragut demonstrated his seamanship and his ability to remain cool in crisis situations. While in Rio de Janeiro, Montevideo, and Buenos Aires, he witnessed many historical events including a state visit of the Emperor Dom Pedro I of Brazil. However, Farragut's eyes were giving him so much trouble that he had to request to be sent home.

Susan Farragut's illness had progressed so that now she was confined to bed or a wheelchair. The Farraguts sought medical treatment for her in Philadelphia but had to leave when an epidemic of cholera broke out in that city. The navy granted the leaves Farragut had to request for medical treatment for his wife and for his own problem with his eyes.

On December 4, 1832, he was ordered to an 18-gun sloop, the *Natchez*, that was sailing to South Carolina to enforce federal laws and collect taxes that the state was challenging. President Andrew Jackson was involved in a dispute with the state over whether the federal government could enforce laws that the state opposed.

Next the *Natchez* was ordered to the Brazil station. Farragut had the reputation of being one of the best and the fairest of the lieutenants in the squadron. He was nicknamed "Little Luff" (luff was another word for lieutenant). He was given another command of a little ten-gun schooner.

When Farragut returned to Norfolk, he was relieved of command because of a general reduction in the navy at that time. Many ships also were retired from active service. For the next four years, Farragut was at home awaiting orders. During that time he took up carpentry and cabinetmaking. His wife required care because she could not walk without aid. Farragut often carried her in his arms.

When he finally received orders to a ship at Pensacola, Florida, Farragut took a leave to visit Mississippi. He saw his youngest sister, Elizabeth, for the first time in more than twenty-five years. He again sailed to Mexican waters where he had the duty to protect American interests. He was in the harbor at Veracruz when French ships attacked a castle. He watched the battle and learned much about the tactics in warfare that he was to put to later use in the American Civil War.

Farragut also learned about the danger of a naval officer expressing an opinion about a foreign nation. Farragut had criticized the French admiral for violating his promise to the Mexican General Santa Anna about the hour he would attack if the Mexicans had not withdrawn. The French officer did not take kindly to the criticism, and the secretary of the navy warned Farragut about talking to the newspapers.

This incident may have been one of the reasons why Farragut was without orders for nearly a year. During this time Susan Farragut's illness became worse. She died on December 27, 1840. Farragut praised his wife's patience during her sixteen years of suffering. One Norfolk woman, commenting on his devotion to his wife, remarked: "When Captain Farragut dies, he should have a monument reaching to the skies, made by every wife in the city contributing a stone."

Two months later, Lieutenant Farragut received orders to be the executive officer on the *U.S.S. Delaware*. This assignment was a promotion to a ship of the line with seventy-four guns and a crew of 820. Using what he had learned from observation of foreign ships, Farragut devised a new way of rigging the sails that was more efficient. Also, he developed a new method of handling the powder boxes so that they could be moved faster.

Now Farragut moved up in rank to commander. This promotion came sixteen years after he had received the rank of lieutenant and nearly thirty years from the date of his first sailing with Captain Porter on the *Essex*. He was just forty years old but he had acquired a great deal of experience. Farragut's reputation grew for his skill in handling his ship during successful and difficult maneuvers while leaving ports.

Farragut's ship was sent to the Brazil station. Farragut had a great interest in Latin America. Generally, the navy had a better understanding of the political developments to the south than other United States departments. Under the Monroe Doctrine, Latin America was in the sphere of influence of the United States and off-limits to the Europeans. The navy was in southern waters to see that France or England did not try to take new colonies while the South American nations were fighting for their independence.

When his ship returned to the United States in 1843, Farragut gave up command in order to go ashore. Overestimating his position, he requested an assignment that would be in a squadron commanded by one of the Perry family. However, the Perrys had not forgotten Farragut's remarks that had hurt a brother's naval career—the incident that had been behind Farragut's failure of his lieutenant's exam. The rejection of his request showed the weakness of Farragut's ability to get the orders he wanted.

With no orders forthcoming, Farragut spent some time in the mountains of Virginia. Here he courted Virginia Dorcas Loyall, the daughter of a Norfolk family. The two were married on December 26, 1843. On October 12, their only child, a boy named Loyall Farragut, was born. The new father made the baby a little hammock that was hung above the mother's bed. Through a system of ropes and pulleys the hammock could be raised and lowered. It was probably at this time that Farragut wrote his autobiography.

Few officers were as qualified as Farragut to serve in the Mexican War, that was declared by Congress in May of 1846. He knew the Mexican people and the language, and had watched the attack on the castle at Veracruz. It was not until March of 1848 that he received command of the *Saratoga*. Unfortunately, Captain Matthew Perry was put in command of the fleet.

In an effort to get to Mexico as soon as possible, Farragut had to set sail with a crew that was 10 percent short of the full number and was not well trained or of the best quality. When he arrived at Veracruz the castle had already been taken by the United States army.

With Perry in command, Farragut was ordered to blockade ports—a boring duty. The poor quality of officers on Farragut's ship almost led to a mutiny by the crew. Perry criticized Farragut for failing to board a steamer that landed a Mexican general. However, Farragut had understood that the army was exercising port control. Perry complained to the secretary of the navy about Farragut.

Then yellow fever broke out on Farragut's ship and he and ninety of the crew were down with the disease. With half his crew, an entire watch, unable to function, Farragut notified Perry of the situation. Perry took no action to get the ship back to Pensacola where the sick could be better treated. Two months later Perry ordered the ship to Veracruz to confirm the report. The ship was held in the harbor for another month without orders to send the ship home. Other ships plagued with yellow fever were sent home promptly. Finally Farragut lost his temper and wrote a letter through channels to the secretary of the navy asking to be relieved of his command so that Perry would grant some relief to his crew.

Perry forwarded the letter with his own minimizing the illness aboard the *Saratoga*, giving incorrect information about the illness in his fleet, and calling attention to the intemperate tone of Farragut's letter. Then twelve days later, Perry ordered the *Saratoga* to return to Pensacola.

The letter damaged Farragut's career. While Perry received important assignments after the war, Farragut drew orders to be executive officer of the Norfolk Navy Yard. It could have been worse for Farragut, but his technical expertise on ships and docks saved him. Nevertheless, this time was a low point in his career.

While working in Norfolk, Farragut came down with cholera and nearly died. But after recuperating he was able to return to duty. An important event during his assignment at Norfolk was the launching of a new steam warship named the *Powatan.*

Farragut was given a new duty in keeping with his interest in improving guns. He was to prepare a book of ordnance regulations. When he had completed that task, he asked for an assignment to observe the guns being used by the French and British in the Crimean War, but the department of the navy took no action on that suggestion. Instead he was ordered to establish a navy yard in the newly acquired territory of California.

His wife and nine-year-old son were to accompany him on the journey west by way of Nicaragua. The trip was hazardous—they traveled through the tropics and found only poor accommodations. Farragut had been ill at the start of the journey and was nursed by his wife. When they reached San Francisco, the family's first home was aboard a ship, then in a small cottage for two years until the commandant's house was finished. In California Farragut's health improved. In 1855 he was commissioned a captain.

San Francisco was a brawling city that in 1856 became divided into two armed camps. Farragut, as the senior naval officer in the area, was drawn into the fight when a naval captain became involved. Farragut did not want to act in a dispute involving state law but stood by to protect federal interests such as safeguarding the four million dollars in gold of the United States Treasury in the San Francisco Mint. His diplomatic handling of the incident was approved by the secretary of the navy and demonstrated Farragut's judgment and prudence that would qualify him for future command posts. By 1858 Farragut's work in building the navy yard was completed and he returned to the East.

The family settled again at Norfolk. Farragut's old enemy Commodore Perry had died. On January 1, 1859 Farragut took command of a new sloop of war, the *Brooklyn*. This ship gave him the opportunity to learn how to maneuver and use a steamship. This sloop was actually larger than one of the old sailing ships of the line. She was equipped with sails, but had a smokestack in the center. Two vertical boilers drove the engines that connected to a drive shaft that turned the screw propeller. Anthracite coal provided the energy. Because so much was still to be learned about this new technology, the ship was able to develop a maximum speed of only eleven knots.

Although the ship performed to Farragut's satisfaction, there were problems with the crew. A seaman became drunk and was fighting and abusive. One of the officers ordered the man to be gagged. Either because of the gag or the intoxication, the sailor died. The crew and civilian authorities were upset at the way the case was handled. The press made it appear that Captain Farragut was the murderer. Farragut answered in an evenhanded way indicating that he was at all times willing to answer to the laws of his country but that he was not guilty of any cruelty.

With the end of his tour of duty on the *Brooklyn*, Farragut moved his family from New York, where his son had been attending school, back to Norfolk. In 1860 he was living in Virginia when there was talk of the Southern states leaving the Union. Farragut became very pessimistic as one after another of the Southern states pulled out. What would he do if Virginia seceded? Virginia was his home and adopted state. It was the native state of his wife and her relatives.

On April 17, 1861, the Virginia convention passed an ordinance of secession by a vote of eighty-five to fifty-five. Farragut was accustomed to talking over news with other naval officers. He learned that most of the others from the South had already sent in their resignations from the United States navy in order to be at the command of the Confederacy. He was told by one of the officers that he must either resign or leave Norfolk.

Farragut went home to tell his wife the news. Farragut did not want to be called to duty by the United States to the Norfolk Navy Yard where he would probably have to fight against his neighbors. He decided to go north that very day. Farragut told his wife that she could choose to accompany him or remain with her family. She decided to go with him and packed the few possessions she could take with her. The Farraguts made their way to Hastings-on-Hudson in New York where they rented a small cottage.

Farragut was sixty years old. Later he was to tell a midshipman that he still felt young and tested it each birthday by turning a handspring. He was an experienced naval officer whose talents the United States would need. But could this Southerner who had elected to fight for the North be trusted?

Chapter 8

BEST UNION OFFICER OF THE CIVIL WAR

Farragut's New York neighbors were suspicious of this Southerner who roamed the hills with nothing to do. The rumor spread that he was a spy who was planning to blow up the Croton Aqueduct to create a water shortage.

The United States navy was in confusion. The Pensacola Navy Yard had surrendered. President Lincoln ordered the Confederate ports to be blockaded. With all the bays and inlets, that meant twelve thousand miles had to be watched. There were only three effective ships to carry out this command since most of the twenty-six steamships and the sixteen sailing ships were scattered around the world.

Farragut wrote to the secretary of the navy to tell him why he had left Norfolk. He executed the oath of allegiance required of all officers in order to determine which ones would be loyal to the Union. He went to Washington to ask for a command of a fast ship to battle a Confederate warship that had run the blockade and was picking off Union shipping. The secretary of the navy was busy trying to get ships together and could not see him. There was little naval action that first summer.

When Farragut was called to duty, it was to serve on a survey board to examine the fitness of officers. It was important duty, but Farragut wanted a command of a ship.

In November 1861 his name was given consideration as commander of a fleet that was to attack New Orleans. The idea for the attack had come from Commander David Porter, the son of Farragut's old mentor who had since died. Some considered Farragut lacking in daring. Some thought him overly enthusiastic. Others were disappointed that this relatively unknown officer would be given such an important command. While the authorities had carefully checked out Farragut's willingness to fight against his Southern friends, many worried about the decision to offer the command to this native Tennessean whose home had been in Virginia.

Farragut was delighted to receive command of the expedition against New Orleans. He had to make adjustments in the ships to permit them to fight on the Mississippi River and to enter the delta. In peacetime, channels had been dredged to keep them open to New Orleans. Now the silt had filled in, making passage of the ships in the channels very difficult. One ship had to be left outside the river, but the older and more diplomatic Farragut made the effort in order to satisfy the "experts" in Washington. Other ships had to be unloaded and dragged by foot through the mud.

Not only the mud, but also complaints by officers who were to take part in the expedition created difficulties in Washington. Commander Porter, who was to be in charge of the mortar flotilla, or bomb fleet, began to play some politics and complain about the delays. Washington lost faith in Farragut, and had there been wireless communications with him Farragut might have been relieved of command.

The route up the Mississippi to New Orleans from the south was protected by Fort Jackson and Fort St. Philip. Two huge chains with old boats and logs formed a barrier across the river at this point. Sharpshooters lined the banks. Above the barrier about a dozen armed Confederate ships and several unarmed craft stood ready to take on the Union force. On April 14, 1862, Farragut began moving his ships upriver.

For two days and nights, the ships bombarded the forts, and the forts fired back. Porter had said that in two days he would demolish the forts. Farragut had been skeptical but held his peace because he knew that the Washington officials were convinced that the forts would fall in that time. At the end of the two day period, Farragut called a meeting of his captains. It was clear that they believed that the forts should be taken before going on to New Orleans.

Farragut thought otherwise. He gave orders for the barricade to be broken and for the ships to proceed past the forts. If they thought that the Confederates would be surprised, they were mistaken. The Confederates sent down a fire ship with flames shooting up above the mast. After some confusion the Union forces were able to tow the boat to shore where it burned itself out. Farragut visited every ship in his command to be sure that his orders were understood. Finally, on the evening of April 24, the Union ships began to move into position for the run past the forts.

The fighting was fierce when the Confederate ships attacked. By 5:30 A.M. the next morning, the battle was over. The Union forces lost 37 men with 149 wounded and there was some damage to the ships. The Confederate losses in the forts were small with only 11 killed and 37 wounded in both forts. The Confederate ships had sustained 73 killed and 73 wounded. Eight of the Confederate ships were destroyed, two fled upriver, and two remained safe under the guns of the fort. The Confederate commander of the river was Farragut's cousin-in-law.

Major-General Benjamin F. Butler, who had orders to assist Farragut with the expedition, wrote to him: "Allow me to congratulate you and your command upon the bold, daring, brilliant, and successful passage of the Forts by your fleet this morning. A more gallant exploit it has never fallen to the lot of man to witness."

Farragut, himself, described his feelings to his wife the next day: "I am so agitated that I can scarcely write, and I shall only tell you that it has pleased Almighty God to preserve my life through a fire such as the world has scarcely known."

The tactic of bypassing a strong point such as a fort and moving along toward the objective was one that the United States was to use in later wars. It was this maneuver that General Douglas MacArthur implemented in World War II when he moved past Japanese strongholds in the Pacific.

New Orleans was alarmed at the news that Farragut had passed the protecting forts. Farragut gave his men a brief rest and declared a day of prayer and thanksgiving. The Confederates at New Orleans made ready for battle. A thousand bales of cotton were burned and set afloat on the river rather than be left for the enemy.

Farragut moved his ships into position to attack the fortifications at New Orleans. After twenty minutes of bombardment, the fight was over. The Confederate guns were either broken, bent, or knocked out. The city was hostile and the city authorities did not want to surrender to the few Union warships that they felt were there because of a "freak of luck." Farragut exercised great patience in trying to negotiate the surrender. Although the mayor refused to lower the flag even in the face of the damage that the ships could do to New Orleans, the matter was resolved when Farragut ordered the marines to march to the customs house and raise the Union flag.

At first the Eastern press gave the credit for the victory over New Orleans to Porter or Butler, who later on knocked out the two forts. Only a week later was the victory known to be Farragut's. Moreover, the full significance of the capture of New Orleans was not appreciated at that time. It was this event that changed the support of many of the European nations away from the Confederacy.

Farragut next moved to take Baton Rouge and Natchez. The heavily fortified Vicksburg was another matter. Lincoln wanted Farragut to take his force to meet a flotilla of Union ships from the north on the Mississippi. Farragut managed to get beyond Vicksburg, but he did not have sufficient manpower or the right kind of ships to clear the river or take and hold Vicksburg. However, on July 1 the two Union flotillas from up and down the river met as Lincoln had wanted. The crews from the two fleets cheered. The Union fleet from the North could blockade Vicksburg. Farragut requested permission to take his ships to the Gulf of Mexico to be used in the blockade there.

Lincoln had asked Congress to thank Farragut and his men for the capture of New Orleans. Two months later in July, Congress acted to create a new rank of rear admiral in the United States navy. David Glasgow Farragut was then commissioned as America's first admiral. He was now the only admiral and the highest-ranking naval officer, though his pay was still $5,000 a year—the same as any captain commanding a squadron. When word of the advancement came to New Orleans, he was saluted by the army and his own ships.

In August Farragut was assigned the duty of blockading the gulf ports of the Confederacy. The many Confederate ships that succeeded in getting through the blockade made this task a difficult one. The Confederates raided Galveston, Texas, and took over the port. A number of Union ships were captured by the Confederates at various places.

Farragut felt that the only way he could slow down the

movement of goods from neutral Mexico and from Texas was to attack Port Hudson—about 135 miles above New Orleans. Port Hudson protected a stretch of the Mississippi and the Red River along which the Confederates received supplies from the southwest. As Farragut's ships moved into battle position, the fleet surgeon suggested that Farragut's son, who had been serving as a civilian clerk to his father, be sent below deck for protection. Farragut declined this special treatment, indicating that although Loyall was his only child and not in the service, his son would act as an aide and help convey his orders during battle.

Victory was not with the Union forces this time. Farragut reported the loss of ships to his fleet. However, in Washington, the fact that the flagship and one gunboat had succeeded in getting past the fire of the fort was enough for Lincoln to declare a victory. It was true that the two Union ships were effective in preventing some steamers from landing supplies at Port Hudson. As Union forces began to win battles along the Mississippi, it was not long before the Confederates could no longer use the river as a highway for their supplies.

Farragut, sick with the fever, and with a ship requiring repair, was granted a furlough to return to the Brooklyn Navy Yard. The crowds came to inspect his ship, the *Hartford*, with its 240 holes from shot and shells hurled at it during the war. Farragut, who had left as an unknown officer, returned as a hero in August of 1863. After recovering for a little over a month in Hastings, Farragut went to Washington.

Farragut called on the Secretary of the Navy Welles, who wrote in his diary: "The more I see and know of Farragut the better I like him. He has the qualities I supposed when he was selected. The ardor and sincerity which struck me during the Mexican War when he wished to take Vera Cruz, with the unassuming and the unpresuming gentleness of a true hero." Moreover Welles recorded some days later a conversation he had with President Lincoln. He reported that Lincoln thought that "there had not been, take it all in all, so good an appointment in either branch of the service as Farragut" and that "no man surpasses Farragut in his estimation."

In October, Farragut returned to action and to the Battle of Mobile Bay. Here Farragut uttered the words for which he is famous: "Damn the torpedoes! Full speed ahead." With the victory at Mobile Bay, he received the thanks of the nation and the praise of Lincoln, Welles, and various generals. Naval officers in Britain and France acknowledged that Farragut was one of the great admirals.

Farragut requested a leave for health reasons and returned to New York where he was given a hero's welcome. He went home to Hastings for a rest. He was back in Washington by mid-January where he attended the opera with the Lincolns. The Farraguts were present for Lincoln's inauguration on March 4.

The Farraguts then made their way down to their old home

in Norfolk for a visit with relatives. Farragut made a quick trip to Richmond after the Confederate capital fell. The Farraguts attended receptions at Norfolk, but were snubbed by some of their old friends because the admiral had chosen to fight for the Union. After a brief visit in Norfolk, Farragut left, never to return.

After the war, the Farraguts traveled a good bit, but finally settled down in New York City. With the money he received from prizes of war (the value of the ships he captured) and from gifts of grateful merchants, the Farraguts bought a town house at 113 East 36th Street. During the winter of 1865 the admiral enjoyed the many dinners and social life that the city offered.

In the summer of 1866, Farragut was promoted from vice admiral to admiral of the navy. Again, he was the first American to hold that rank.

In the spring of 1867, Farragut was appointed to command the European Squadron on a goodwill cruise of that area. In 1867, Farragut was again sent to Europe—this time with Mrs. Farragut, thanks to a waiver of naval regulations against wives accompanying their husbands. They were honored in France, Germany, Russia, Sweden, Denmark, Portugal, Spain, Italy, Holland, Belgium, and even England, a nation that had sympathized with the Confederates. Often they dined with emperors and kings.

Nowhere was he received more warmly than in Spain where

he was welcomed by Queen Isabella, who took special notice of his Spanish ancestry. He visited Minorca and citizens from Ciudadella, the birthplace of his father, called on him. He spent two days in that town. It was said that he could have been elected governor of the islands or king of Spain. He was made a citizen of Ciudadella and given the registry of the baptism of his father.

Farragut had no political ambitions, even when approached on this cruise by political bosses about running for the presidency of the United States. Some had speculated that Farragut was on a diplomatic mission to conclude treaties with some of the countries that he visited. However, the cruise was exactly what it appeared to be—a goodwill mission that was highly successful.

One advantage of this seventeen-month world tour was that it kept the Farraguts out of range of the animosity surrounding the impeachment trial of President Andrew Johnson and the election of General Ulysses S. Grant. In the summer of 1869 the Farraguts traveled back to California to see the completion of the Mare Island Navy Yard. On their way home from California, the admiral had a heart attack in Chicago. His son was called, but the father rallied and was able to return home.

His health continued to fail gradually. His physician suggested that he leave New York during the summer and go to Portsmouth, New Hampshire. The navy department made available to Farragut and his wife a dispatch steamer to take them to New Hampshire. Farragut realized that his end was near. He left his bed, dressed in full uniform, and went up on deck to take the salute as his ship entered Portsmouth. One day in the naval yard, he walked around an old sailing sloop and remarked to the sailor in charge: "This is the last time I shall ever tread the deck of a man-of-war." A few days later he was too sick to leave his bed, and in two weeks he died of a paralytic stroke. It was August 14, 1870. Farragut was sixty-nine years old.

His black steward, John H. Brooks, recorded Farragut's death in his diary: "My good friend Admiral D.G. Farragut died yesterday. What a great loss he is to this country. Thank God he died in peace with his Maker. I have lost my best naval friend."

The naval yard staff united with the Farragut family's friends in a funeral service of the Episcopal church, followed by Masonic honors, and the military salute. The coffin was placed in a temporary vault until autumn when the remains were to be removed to Annapolis for burial.

The public was unhappy with the lack of more official government recognition of the death of their hero. With Mrs. Farragut's consent, the coffin was removed to a cemetery in New York with President Grant and the Cabinet attending the funeral. However, it rained torrents that drenched the uniforms and clothing of those in the solemn procession in New York.

Farragut served as an example to others who came after him. Admiral George Dewey, who had been with Farragut in the New Orleans campaign as a lieutenant, wrote to Loyall Farragut about his own naval victory in Manila Bay years later: "In all my operations in the Philippines, the example of the Great Admiral, your father, was constantly before me. I often said to myself in great emergencies, 'What would Farragut have done under like emergencies?' And when I entered Manila Bay immediately on arriving off the coast, I felt sure I was doing exactly as he would have done."

Loyall Farragut wrote of his father's attitude toward war: "When actually engaged in battle, he always seemed to enjoy the conflict, and yet there was a gentle and sentimental side to his nature. I have heard him remark with sadness: 'War is a terrible business. It is demoralizing and brings out all the worst characteristics of men; but', he added, 'we must go to war, or more terrible things may follow.'"

The son of Spain and boy of the American frontier, who went to sea as a midshipman at age ten, served his country well through the War of 1812, the Mexican War, and the Civil War, and through the difficult times of peace when the navy tends to be forgotten.

The funeral procession of Admiral Farragut proceeds up
Broadway in New York City.

GLOSSARY

BALEARIC ISLANDS. A group of islands off Spain in the Mediterranean Sea. George Farragut, Admiral Farragut's father, was born there and the admiral visited these islands on his triumphal tour after the Civil War.

BATTERY CASEMENT. The openings on a ship for the guns

BEAM. The widest point of the ship

BOAT. A small, open vessel propelled on water by oars, sails, or engine. Large vessels are called ships.

BOAT KETCH. A two-master sailing ship with one or two large guns mounted on clear deck space ahead of the mainmast.

BRIG. A two-master ship with square sails or a jail on a United States warship.

BROADSIDES. The whole side of a ship above the waterline, all the guns that can be fired from one side of a ship, or the firing together of all the guns from one side of a ship.

CASEMENT. A hinged frame over an opening that opens outward

CONVOY. An escort to protect ships

COXSWAIN. A person who steers a boat

CUTLASS. A short, thick, curved sword with one cutting edge that sailors used to carry.

FLAGSHIP. A ship that carries the commander of a fleet or squadron and flies his or her flag.

FLOTILLA. A small fleet of boats or ships.

FORECASTLE. The part of the upper deck of a ship that is forward of the foremast.

FOREMAST. The mast for holding sails that is nearest the front or bow of the ship.

FRIGATE. A fast, medium-sized sailing warship that carried 28 to 60 guns.

GROG. An alcoholic beverage, originally rum diluted with water

HARDTACK. Unleavened bread in hard, large wafers

HAZING. A process of initiating or disciplining someone by means of practical jokes, tricks, or humiliating ordeals.

IRONCLAD. A warship with thick iron plates for armor.

KEEL. A piece of timber or plate that runs lengthwise along the center of the bottom of the ship.

KEEL OVER. Overturn, capsize

MAJORCA. The largest of the Balearic Islands in the Mediterranean near Spain

MARQUESAS. A group of French islands in the South Pacific

MIDSHIPMAN. The lowest class of officer in the United States navy at the time that Admiral Farragut lived; now a student in training for the rank of ensign in the United States navy.

MINORCA. One of the Balearic Islands in the Mediterranean near Spain

MIZZEN. The fore and aft sail set on the mizzenmast that is the mast closest to the back or stern of the ship.

MONITOR. An armored ship, or ironclad, with a low, flat deck and heavy guns fitted in one or more revolving turrets, named after the first Union ship of this type, the *Monitor*, that fought a Confederate ship, the *Merrimac* also named the *Virginia*, in the first battle of ironclads on March 9, 1862.

PORT. Left-hand side of a ship as one faces forward toward the bow, the front of the ship.

PRIMER. A small top or tube containing explosives that is used to fire the main charge of a gun or mine (or torpedo).

PRIVATEER. A privately owned and operated ship that is authorized by a warring nation to attack and capture enemy ships.

REPUBLICANISM. The form of government in which the supreme power is in all the citizens entitled to vote, as opposed to monarchies where power is vested in the king or queen and to other forms of government where power is located other than with all the citizens.

RIGGING. The chains and ropes that are used to support and work the masts, sails, and other such equipment on a ship

SHALLOW-DRAFT. A small depth of water that a ship draws or displaces: a shallow-draft boat could go closer to a shoreline.

SHIP OF THE LINE. A seventeenth or eighteenth-century powerful fighting ship named because of the tactic of fighting naval battles in a line formation.

SHEET. A rope or chain that is attached to a lower corner of a sail to control the sail.

SLOOP. A small fore and aft rigged sailing ship with one mast. Later when the term was applied to warships, it referred to sailing ships rigged in several ways, and larger than a gunboat.

SPANISH ARMADA. A Spanish fleet sent by Philip II of Spain in 1588 against England and defeated by the English fleet.

SQUALL. A violent windstorm usually accompanied by rain or snow.

STARBOARD. The right-hand side of the ship as one faces toward the bow, the front of the ship.

STEERAGE. Originally, the part of the ship containing the steering mechanism: it is the least desirable part of the ship for passengers.

TACKLES. The rigging and pulleys used to operate the sails.

TERRAPIN. Various species of turtles found in fresh or salt water.

TOPMAST. The second horizontal mast above the deck of a sailing ship, supported by the lower mast and often supporting a topgallant mast above.

TORPEDO. A metal case containing an explosive, such as an underwater mine.

WEEVILS. Beetles, the larvae or young of which are destructive to food and crops.

WHEEL CHAINS. Lines that connect the wheel to the steering mechanism.

WHERRY. A light rowboat that can be used to move passengers from ship to shore.

YARD. A slender rod, tapering toward the ends, fastened at right angles across a mast to support a sail.

A bronze statue of Admiral Farragut by
Augustus Saint-Gaudens

David Glasgow Farragut 1801-70

1801 David Glasgow Farragut is born on July 5 in East Tennessee. Thomas Jefferson is inaugurated as president of the U.S. The first iron trolley tracks are laid in Great Britain.

1802 Horse racing is introduced in Britain. A German naturalist, Gottfried Treviranus, coins the term "biology."

1803 U.S. buys a large tract of land from the Gulf of Mexico to the northwest including Louisiana, from France (Louisiana Purchase). Robert Fulton propels a boat by steam power.

1804 Alexander Hamilton, former U.S. secretary of the treasury, is killed in a duel with Vice-president Aaron Burr. Soldiers Meriwether Lewis and William Clark begin an exploration of the western United States.

1805 Jefferson begins his second term as president. Britain and U.S. break over trade with the West Indies.

1806 Lewis and Clark complete their exploration.

1807 The Farragut family moves to New Orleans, Louisiana. Aaron Burr is tried for treason and acquitted. The U.S. places an embargo on any ships sailing from the U.S. to foreign ports. Fulton's steamboat, the *Clermont*, navigates on the Hudson River. Charles and Mary Lamb write *Tales from Shakespeare*.

1808 Farragut's mother dies. U.S. prohibits importation of slaves. Extensive excavations begin at Pompeii, Italy. Pigtails in men's hair disappear from fashion.

1809 Farragut goes to live with Commander David Porter. James Madison becomes the fourth president of the U.S.

1810 Farragut becomes a midshipman in the U.S. navy. The first public billiard rooms open in London.

1811 Young Farragut becomes a midshipman on the *Essex*. William Henry Harrison, later president of the U.S., defeats Indians at Tippecanoe, Indiana. Johan Meyer, a Swiss mountaineer, climbs the Jungfrau, Switzerland.

1812 U.S. declares war on Britain. A machine is invented for spinning flax. Fairy Tales by the Grimm Brothers is published.

1813 War of 1812 continues. Mexico declares itself independent. The waltz conquers European ballrooms.

1814 Treaty of Ghent ends the War of 1812 on December 24. Francis Scott Key writes the poem The Star-Spangled Banner. The London Times is printed by a steam-operated press. St. Margaret's, Westminster, London, is the first district to be illuminated by gas. The first successful steam locomotive is built by George Stephenson.

1815 The first steam warship, the U.S.S. Fulton, is built. American ships and prisoners held by pirates of the Barbary Coast (Morocco, Algeria, and Tunisia) are freed by U.S. navy captain Stephen Decatur.

1816 Sir David Brewster invents the kaleidoscope. Economic crisis in Britain causes widespread immigration to Canada and the U.S.

1817 James Monroe inaugurated as fifth president of the U.S. U.S. begins construction of Erie Canal. The University of Virginia, designed by Thomas Jefferson, is built.

1818 The U.S. and Britain agree to the boundary (the 49th parallel) between Canada and the U.S. The *Savannah* becomes the first steamship to cross the Atlantic (26 days).

1820 Farragut takes the examination for the rank of lieutenant. The Missouri Compromise allows the state of Maine to enter the Union as a free state while Missouri becomes a slave state. Rich deposits of platinum are discovered in Utah. Washington Colonization Society founds Liberia for repatriation of blacks.

1821 Farragut, on the second attempt, qualifies as a lieutenant. James Monroe begins second term as president of the U.S.

1822 Farragut is ordered aboard the *John Adams* for service in Mexico. The streets of Boston are lit by gas. The world's first iron railroad bridge is built in England.

1823 Farragut obtains command of the *Ferret*. Mexico becomes a republic. The Monroe Doctrine closes the American continent to colonization by European powers. Charles MacIntosh patents a waterproof fabric.

1824 Farragut marries Susan Caroline Merchant. The Erie Canal is finished.

1825 Farragut becomes a lieutenant and is assigned to transport the Marquis de Lafayette home to France aboard the *Brandywine*. John Quincy Adams inaugurated as sixth president of the U.S. A baseball club is organized at Rochester, New York. Horse-drawn buses carry passengers in London.

1826 Farragut takes a leave of absence to care for his ill wife.

1827 Joseph Niepce produces photographs on a metal plate. Karl Baedeker begins publishing his travel guides. George Ohm formulates Ohm's Law, defining electrical current potential and resistance.

1828 Farragut is assigned to the *Vandalia*, which set sail for Brazil. Construction begins on the Baltimore & Ohio Railroad, the first railroad in the U.S. to carry passengers and freight. Noah Webster writes *American Dictionary of the English Language.*

1829 Andrew Jackson is inaugurated as seventh president of the U.S. Slavery is abolished in Mexico. Louis-Jacques-Mandé Daguerre forms a partnership with Niepce for the development of their photographic inventions. Louis Braille publishes a raised alphabet for the blind. James Smithson dies and bequeaths his fortune to found the Smithsonian Institution in Washington, D.C. The first Oxford-Cambridge boat race takes place at Henley, England. A centralized police force is installed in London.

1830 The Royal Geographic Society is founded in Britain. Charles Lyell, Scottish geologist, divides the geological system into three groups that he names Eocene, Miocene, and Pliocene. Evangelist Joseph Smith writes the *Book of Mormon.*

1831 Farragut returns to Norfolk to defend the naval yard against a possible attack by Nat Turner, a black preacher who led an uprising of slaves. Charles Darwin sails aboard the H.M.S. *Beagle* as naturalist on a surveying expedition to South America, Australia, and New Zealand. James Clark Ross reaches the magnetic North Pole. Michael Faraday carries out a series of experiments demonstrating the discovery of electromagnetic induction. London Bridge is opened. The first horse-drawn buses appear in New York.

1832 Farragut is ordered to the *Natchez* sailing to South Carolina to enforce federal laws. The word "socialism" comes into use in English and in French. The manufacture of friction matches is well established in Europe. The New England Anti-Slavery Society is founded in Boston.

1833 Andrew Jackson begins his second term as president of the U.S. Slavery is abolished in the British Empire. K.F. Gauss and W.E. Weber devise the electromagnetic telegraph, which functions over a distance of 9,000 feet.

1834 Farragut takes command of the *Boxer* and sails to Brazil and back. Abraham Lincoln, at 25, enters politics as assemblyman in the Illinois legislature. Cyrus McCormick patents a harvesting machine. The first American organization of amateur rowing clubs is founded in New York. Walter Hunt of New York constructs one of the first sewing machines.

1835 The New York Herald newspaper is founded. Texas declares its right to secede from Mexico. Halley's Comet reappears. The first burglar-proof safe is patented. William Henry Fox Talbot takes the first negative photograph.

1836 Texas wins its independence from Mexico and declares itself a republic.

1837 Martin Van Buren is inaugurated as eighth president of the U.S. Samuel Morse exhibits his electric telegraph in New York. A financial and economic panic hits the U.S. Nathaniel Hawthorne's Twice Told Tales is published.

1838 The Underground Railroad for escaped slaves is organized. The steamer Sirius sails from London to New York in 15 days.

1839 Charles Goodyear makes possible the commercialization of rubber by developing the process of vulcanization. The first bicycle is constructed by a Scotsman, Kirkpatrick Macmillan. The first baseball game is played in Cooperstown, New York.

1840 Farragut's wife dies. The game of ninepins becomes popular in America.

1841 Farragut is commissioned a commander and becomes executive officer of the *Delaware.* William Henry Harrison dies one month after his inauguration as ninth president of the U.S. Vice-president John Tyler succeeds him.

1842 An American physician, Crawford Long, uses ether to produce surgical anesthesia. American naval officer Matthew Maury begins his researches in oceanography. Boston and Albany are connected by a railroad. *The Masque of the Red Death* by Edgar Allan Poe is published.

1843 Farragut returns to the U.S. He marries Virginia Loyall. China and the U.S. sign first treaty of peace, amity, and commerce. Skiing begins as a sport. Congress grants Samuel Morse $30,000 to build a telephone line from Washington to Baltimore.

1844 Texas annexation plan rejected by U.S Senate. The modern cooperative movement begins in England. Woodpulp paper is invented.

1845 James Polk is inaugurated as the eleventh president of the U.S. The U.S. Naval Academy at Annapolis, Maryland, is founded. The Knickerbocker Baseball Club codifies the rules of the game. An American dentist, W.F. Morton, uses ether as an anesthetic.

1846 U.S. declares war on Mexico. Brigham Young leads the Mormons from Nauvoo City, Illinois, to Salt Lake City, Utah. Elias Howe patents the sewing machine.

1847 Gold discoveries in California lead to the first gold rush. British Factory Act restricts the working day for women and children.

1848 Farragut receives control of the *Saratoga*. War with Mexico ends. U.S. gets Texas, New Mexico, California, Utah, Nevada, Arizona, and parts of Colorado and Wyoming in return for large indemnity.

1849 Zachary Taylor becomes twelfth president of the U.S. French physicist Armand Fizeau measures the speed of light. Walter Hunt patents the safety pin.

1850 Henry Clay's compromise slavery resolutions are laid before U.S. Senate. President Zachary Taylor dies. Vice-president Millard Fillmore becomes thirteenth president.

1851 Isaac Singer devises the continuous-stitch sewing machine. The first double-decker bus is introduced. *Moby Dick* by Herman Melville is published.

1852 A suspension bridge is built across Niagara Falls. Wells, Fargo Company is founded. Harriet Beecher Stowe's book about slavery, *Uncle Tom's Cabin,* is published.

1853 Franklin Pierce is inaugurated as fourteenth president of the U.S. Alexander Wood uses hypodermic syringe for subcutaneous injections. Vaccination against smallpox is made compulsory in Britain.

1854 Farragut goes to California to establish a navy yard. Republican party is formed in the U.S. Commodore M.C. Perry negotiates first American-Japanese treaty. German watchmaker Heinrich Goebel invents first form of electric light bulb.

1855 Farragut becomes a captain. First iron Cunard steamer crosses the Atlantic in nine and a half days. Florence Nightingale introduces hygienic standards into military hospitals during Crimean War. *Leaves of Grass* by Walt Whitman is published.

1856 Sir Henry Bessemer introduces converter in his process for making steel. Big Ben, a 13.5-ton bell, is mounted at the British House of Parliament.

1857 James Buchanan inaugurated as fifteenth president of the U.S. Pasteur proves that fermentation is caused by living organisms. Financial and economic crisis throughout Europe is precipitated by speculation in U.S. railroad shares. Otis installs the first safety elevator.

1858 Farragut completes work of building navy yard in San Francisco. Suez Canal Company is formed. Joseph Lister studies coagulation of blood.

1859 Farragut takes command of the steamship *Brooklyn*. The first practical storage battery is invented. George Pullman designs the Pullman railroad cars. Work on the Suez Canal begins.

1860 Abraham Lincoln elected sixteenth president of the U.S. South Carolina secedes from the Union in protest. Baseball becomes popular in New York and Boston.

1861 Washington Peace Convention tries to preserve the Union, but the Confederate States of America is formed with South Carolina, Georgia, Alabama, Mississippi, Florida, and Louisiana. Virginia convention passes ordinance of secession. Confederates take Fort Sumter, South Carolina, beginning the Civil War. Farragut receives command of expedition against New Orleans. Lincoln calls for militia to suppress Confederacy.

1862 Farragut engages in battle with Confederate ships in New Orleans; he becomes a rear admiral. Lincoln issues Emancipation Proclamation to be effective January 1, 1863: all slaves held in rebelling territory declared free. Léon Foucault successfully measures the speed of light. Two ironclad ships, the *Monitor* and the *Merrimac* (*Virginia*), battle in Hampton Roads, Virginia. U.S. issues legal paper money.

1863 Lincoln gives his Gettysburg Address at dedication of a military cemetery. Construction is begun on the London Underground railroad.

1864 Farragut, directing his ships in Mobile Bay, says, "Damn the torpedoes! Full speed ahead." Farragut is commissioned a vice admiral. General William Tecumseh Sherman marches through Georgia, defeats Confederate army in Atlanta and occupies Savannah. "In God We Trust," first appears on U.S coins. Abraham Lincoln is reelected president. The International Red Cross is founded in Switzerland.

1865 The Farraguts move to New York City. Confederate states surrender at Appomattox Court House, Virginia, to end Civil War. Abraham Lincoln is assassinated; he is succeeded by Vice-president Andrew Johnson. Thirteenth Amendment to U.S. constitution abolishes slavery. Atlantic cable is completed.

1866 Farragut becomes admiral of the navy. Fourteenth Amendment to U.S. constitution prohibits voting discrimination, denies government office to certain Civil War rebels, and repudiates Confederate war debts. Alfred Nobel invents dynamite.

1867 Farragut goes on an extended cruise in European waters. British North America Act establishes Dominion of Canada. Russia sells Alaska to U.S for $7,200,000.

1868 U.S. President Andrew Johnson is impeached for allegedly violating Tenure-of-Office Act, but is acquitted by Senate. The first professional baseball club, the Cincinnati Red Stockings, is founded. *Little Women* by Louisa May Alcott is published.

1869 General Ulysses S. Grant is inaugurated as eighteenth president of the U.S. The first transcontinental railroad in the U.S. is formed when the Union Pacific and the Central Pacific are joined in Utah. The Suez Canal opens. Dmitry Mendeleyev formulates his periodic law for the classification of the elements.

1870 Admiral Farragut dies on August 14 in Portsmouth, New Hampshire; a public funeral is held in New York on September 30.

Alden, James, 11, 13-14
Alert, surrender of, 36-37
American Man-of-War, **54-55**
American Revolution, George Farragut in, 20
Atlantic Coastal Squadron, 33
Bainbridge, Commodore, 61
Balearic Islands, 7, 19, 70
Barbary pirates, 61
Barclay, 41
Baton Rouge, Louisiana, 85
Blount, William, 20
Brady, Merrill, 23-24
Brandywine, 69, 70
Brazil, 74
Brooklyn, 11, 13, 15, 78-79
Brooks, John H., 91
Buchanan, Buck, 12, 16, 17, 18
Butler, Benjamin F., 84, 85
Cape Horn, **34,** 39, 45
Charleston, South Carolina, 20
Charles X, King (France), 69
Chickasaw, 10
Civil War, 81-82; Battle of Mobile Bay in, 7-18, 88; use of torpedoes in, 7-8, 11, 15; Battle of New Orleans in, 11, 82-85; attack on Port Hudson, 87; and Virginia's secession from Union, 79
Craven, Captain, 14
Creighton, Captain, 61-62
Crimean War, 77
Decatur, Stephen, 61
Delaware, U.S.S., 73
Dewey, Admiral George, 92
Dom Pedro I, Emperor (Brazil), 71
Downes, Captain, 42
Downes, Lieutenant, 33
Ericsson, John, 9
Essex, 28, 31, **53;** motto of, 46; storm damage of, 32-33; surrender of, 49-50; in War of 1812, 35-43, 45-52
Europe, goodwill mission to, 89-90
Evans, Samuel, 65
Farragut, David Glasgow: in Battle of Mobile Bay, 7-18, 88; father of, 7; mother of, 7, 19-20, 20-25; opinion of, on ironclad ships, 9; Lincoln's opinion of, 18, 86, 87; birth of, 21; name change of, 21, 27; siblings of, 22, 24, 66, 73; move to New Orleans, 23-24;

informal adoption by David Porter, Jr., 25-26; feelings for David Porter, Jr., 26; journal writings of, 26, 30, 39; visit to father, 26; move to Washington, 26, 27; as midshipman on *Essex,* 27-33, 36-40; dislike of British, 27, 35; description of, 28, 29, 51; education of, 29, 32, 51, 62, 70; relationship with fellow crew members, 30-31; training of, 31-32; in War of 1812, 33-52; role of, in surrender of *Alert,* 36-37; visit to Porter home, 37; initiation of, into Noble Order of Neptune, 38-39; dislike for tobacco, 39; in Galapagos Islands, 40; as prize master of *Barclay,* 41-42; actions of, during British attack on *Essex,* 48-50; as British prisoner, 50; fight over "Murphy," 50; parole of, 50-51; return to Chester, Pennsylvania, 51; appointment to *Spark,* 51-52, 63-64; and drinking, 52, 61; as captain's aide on *Independence,* 61; aboard *Washington,* 61-62; in Tunis, 62-63; eye trouble of, 63, 70, 71; as captain's aide on *Franklin,* 63; examination of, for rank of lieutenant, 64-66; effect of Perry incident on, 64, 74-75, 75-76; in Norfolk, Virginia, 66-67, 70-71, 72, 75, 76-77, 78, 79; on *John Adams,* 66; on *Greyhound,* 66; on *Ferret,* 67; bouts with yellow fever, 67, 76, 87; first marriage of, 67-68; commission of, as lieutenant, 68-69; on the *Brandywine,* 69; in New York, 70; in New Haven, Connecticut, 70; first wife's illness, 70-73; teaching of boys in service by, 70-71; on *Vandalia,* 71; on *Natchez,* 72; nickname of, 72; relief of command, 72; death of first wife, 73; on *Delaware,* 73; promotion to commander, 74; in Brazil, 74; in Virginia, 75; second marriage of, 75; birth of son, 75; in Mexican War, 75-76, 88; as commander of *Saratoga,* 75-76; at Norfolk Navy Yard, 76-77; bout with cholera, 77; at navy yard in California, 77-78; commission of, as captain, 77; handling of state law dispute, 78; as commander of *Brooklyn*, 78-79; and death of seaman under command of, 78-79; and secession of Virginia, 79; and decision to leave Norfolk, 79-80; in Civil War, 81-88; as commander of expedition against New Orleans, 82-85; and capture of New Orleans, 85; commission of, as admiral, 86; and blockading of gulf ports of Confederacy, 86; attack of, on Port Hudson, 87; return of, to Brooklyn Navy Yard, 87; last visit of, to Norfolk, 89; in New York City, 89; promotion from vice admiral to admiral of navy, 89; goodwill mission of, to Europe, 89-90; in Spain, 89-90; heart attack of, 90; death and funeral of, 91; George Dewey's opinion of, 92; attitude of, toward war, 92

Farragut, David Glasgow (illustrations): **2**, **44**; during Battle of Mobile Bay, **58**; goodwill tour to Europe, **59**; during Civil War, **60**; funeral procession for, **94**; statue of, **98**

Farragut, George, Sr. (father): name change of, 19; birth of, 19; father of, 19; education of, 19; naval career of, 19-20, 23; in American Revolution, 20; as privateer, 20; marriage of, 20-21; and birth of William, 21; and building of home, 21; and birth of James Glasgow, 21; anger and reaction to Indian attack on family, 22-23; and birth of Elizabeth, 24; and wife's death, 25; and retirement of, from navy, 25; and friendship with Porters, 25-26; and visits by Glasgow, 26

Ferragut, Jorge Antonio Magin. *See* Farragut, George, Sr.

Farragut, Elizabeth (sister), 24, 73

Farragut, Elizabeth Shine (mother): marriage of, 20; birth of, 21; family of, 21; Indian attack on, 21; move to New Orleans, 23-24; birth of Elizabeth, 24; birth of James Glasgow, 21; birth of William, 21; death of, 25

Farragut, George (brother), 22

Farragut, Loyall (son), 75, 87, 90, 92

Farragut, Nancy (sister), 22, 67

Farragut, Susan Caroline Merchant (first wife), 66; marriage of, 67-68; illness of, 70, 71-72; death of, 73

Farragut, Virginia Dorcas Loyall (second wife), 75, 89, 91

Farragut, William (brother): birth of, 21; naval appointment of, 25

Ferret, 67

Folsom, Charles, 62

Fort Gaines, 10

Fort Jackson, 83

Fort Morgan, 10, 13

Fort St. Philip, 83

Franklin, 63

Galapagos Islands, 40

Galveston, Texas, 86

George III, King (England), 20

Grant, Ulysses S., 90, 91

Greyhound, 66

Gunboat No. 13, 23

Hamilton, Paul, 27

Hartford, 11, 13, 15, 16, 17, 87

Hillyar, James, 45-48

impressment of sailors, 31

Independence, 61

ironclad ships, in Civil War, 8-11

Isabella, Queen (Spain), 90

Jackson, Andrew, 72

John Adams, 66

Johnson, Andrew, 90

Johnston, J. D., 17

Jones, Richard B., 63

Lackawanna, 17

Lafayette, 69

Lincoln, Abraham, 85-86, 88; opinion of Farragut, 7, 18; and Louisiana Purchase, 23; inaugural ball of, **59**

MacArthur, Douglas, 84

Madison, James, 27

Manhattan, 10, 14

Mare Island Navy Yard, 90

Marquesas, 42

Merrimac, **56**; battle between *Monitor* and, **56**; renaming as *Virginia*, 8; sinking of, 8

Mexican War, Farragut in, 75-76, 88

midshipman: life of, 29, 30, 32; uniform of, 29

Minerva, 35

Minorca, 19-20
Mobile Bay, Battle of, 7-18, **58**, 88
Monitor, 8; battle between, and
  Merrimac, **56**; description of, 9
Monongahela, 17
Monroe Doctrine, 74
Natchez, 72, 85
Nautilus, 33
New Haven, Connecticut, 70
New Orleans: battle at, 11; capture
  of, **57**; levee at, **53**; significance of
  capture of, 85
New York City, 70, 89
Noble Order of Neptune, 38
Norfolk, Virginia, 66, 70-71, 72, 77,
  78, 89
Norfolk Navy Yard, 76-77, 79
Perry, Christopher Raymond, drinking
  problem of, 64
Perry, Matthew, 75-76, 78
Phoebe, motto of, 46
Pontchartrain, Lake, 24, 26
Port-au-Prince, Haiti, 20
Porter, David, Sr., death of, 24-25
Porter, David, Jr., **44, 57**; informal
  adoption of Farragut, 25-26; and
  move to Washington, 26, 27; as
  commander of *Essex,* 28-33, 35-43,
  45-49; and training of men, 31, 43;
  in War of 1812, 35-43, 45-52; visit
  home by, 37; challenge to, from
  British Captain Yeo, 38; discipline of,
  42-43; at Battle of Valparaiso, 45-48;
  and appointment of Farragut to
  Spark, 51-52; approach of, to
  seamanship, 62; son of, 82, 83, 85
Porter, David, III, 82, 83, 85
Port Hudson, 87
Powatan, 77
Randall, Captain, 41-42
Rochelle, James H., 9
Rodgers, George Washington, 33,
  64-65
Santa Anna, 73
Saratoga, 75-76
Selma, 9
Southampton, 38
Spain, 89-90
Spanish Armada, 19
Spark, 52, 63, 64

Taylor, William, 61
Tecumseh, 10, 12, 13; sinking of, 14
Tennessee, 9-10, 11, 14, 15-16; attack on,
  17; surrender of, 17-18
torpedoes, use of, in Civil War, 7-8, 11, 15
Tunis, Tunisia, 62
uniform, of midshipman, 29
Utrecht, Treaty of (1713), 19
Valparaiso, Cuba: battle at, 45-50;
  neutrality of, during War of 1812,
  45, 48
Vandalia, 71
Vesuvius, 27
Vicksburg, Mississippi, 85
Virginia, 8, **56**
War of 1812: Battle of Valparaiso in,
  45-50; beginning of, 33; *Essex* in,
  35-43, 45-52; propaganda warfare in,
  46; surrender of *Alert* in, 36
Washington, D.C., 51, 62
Welles, as secretary of navy, 88
Winnebago, 10
World War II, 84
Yeo, James, 38

About the Author

Leila Merrell Foster is a lawyer, a United Methodist minister, and a clinical psychologist with degrees from Northwestern University and Garrett Evangelical Theological Seminary. She is the author of books and articles on a variety of subjects.

In her travels in the United States and South America, Ms. Foster has seen monuments to David Glasgow Farragut. However, as she researched this biography, she was surprised to learn how often Farragut had taken part in events that had historical significance in the development of the United States. From the young midshipman in the War of 1812 to the first Admiral of the United States navy, Farragut led an exciting life in the service of his country.